The Open University from Within

The Open University from Within

John Ferguson

Dean and Director of Studies in Arts
The Open University

UNIVERSITY OF LONDON PRESS LTD

ISBN 0 340 17965 1

University of London Press Ltd
St Paul's House, Warwick Lane, London EC4P 4AH

Printed in Great Britain by
W & J Mackay Limited, Chatham

Contents

For

AARON (*and* MARINA), ARNOLD (*and* MARGOT), ARTHUR, GERALD (*and* DINAH), GODFREY (*and* DO)

With Thanks

Introduction

When Professor Niblett invited me to write a book under the title *The Open University from Within*, my first thought and plan was to produce a detached and balanced survey after a series of interviews with my colleagues in other faculties. Second thoughts prevailed. It is surprisingly difficult to arrange meetings with one's senior colleagues: they are busy and I am busy, and the time available for writing would not wait on our mutual availability. Further, that would not have fulfilled my title, for much of that could have been done by anyone from outside. It seemed better to make this a genuinely personal picture. I hope that it is not too misleading an account of the work of my colleagues; I portray it as it looks, and errors of emphasis are part of the story of the Open University since they indicate a failure of communication within our structure. I have tried not to neglect any important aspect of the University, but I have treated at greater length those areas I know best, notably the Arts Faculty, not because I think them more important, but because there I can give a more authoritative and immediate picture. Because this is a personal account, I have not been afraid to personalize it, as we have grown used to personalizing our University work; indeed for the very reason and to emphasize the point, I have made the first chapter one of personal reminiscence.

I have written this in odd moments snatched from a busy schedule. I may well have omitted matters which I should have treated. I hope the facts are right; where I have relied on memory, I have qualified an assertion which might be too dogmatic. There is some untidiness, and in particular some repetition where the same topic appropriately appears in different chapters. I have pruned the more offensive examples of this in revision, but some remain, either where I have wanted to reinforce a point, or where the same point seems appropriate in different places.

Jeremy Tunstall's book *The Open University Opens* appeared while I was tidying up my own manuscript, and I was gratefully able to seize on one or two points I had missed, and filch an odd epigram. I have characterized my grosser borrowings by the simple designation 'Tunstall' with a page reference. It is uneven, as a collection of papers from divers hands is bound to be. But I was appalled to find how dully some of us in the OU still write after three years of the OU, and somewhat surprised to find a couple of quite wrong factual statements. (A rash comment; it will lead to scrutiny of my own text, and, I dare say, the unearthing of similar error.) Tunstall's own introduction is a masterly summation of the main innovatory points in the OU, and there is an excellent political history of the University written from outside by Brian MacArthur of *The Times Higher Education Supplement*. For the rest I valued most the concise and candid statements from students; it is strange that there is nothing from the part-time tutors and counsellors. A handy bibliography indicates a surprising paucity of significant writing about the OU. Tunstall's collection is by a long way the most significant item yet to appear.

On 1 January 1974 I went on study leave. I have not therefore been in touch with developments since that date. Any survey of this kind must have a cut-off point; on all grounds it has seemed best not to attempt to carry the story beyond the end of 1973. There have been some changes and reappraisals; there will always be.

I owe a formal debt of gratitude to the Open University for permission to publish some of the statistical tables and other statistics, not here presented in tabular form, but gleaned from the research directed by Naomi McIntosh, and for other material under OU copyright such as the map of the regions and the extract from Lord Crowther's address.

Much of my information has of course been derived from internal documents; it has become a part of me and is not always traceable. I am grateful to those colleagues who have allowed me to pester them with questions, fleshing out casual views with facts.

Among many other debts of gratitude I owe four outstandingly. One to Roy Niblett for the original invitation and for his friendly and constructive encouragement. One to Walter Perry, Vice-Chancellor of the Open University, who kindly offered to read the book in typescript, correct the grosser errors and ensure that I was not misusing confidential material. He is, however, in no sense responsible for what appears here. One to Joyce Anlezark, my secretary and friend, for volunteering to undertake the typing of an untidy manuscript, and doing it with skill and patience. One to my wife Elnora for all that she has contributed to making the Arts Faculty a place where wives and husbands are welcome, and in particular for her continuing high professionalism as (in a double sense, both strict) an amateur indexer. Alongside all these is an intense sense of gratitude for the opportunity of sharing in this thrilling enterprise, and to my colleagues for making it such a delightful experience.

J.F.

CHAPTER ONE

Certain Personal Matters

The Boeing 707 from New York to London shuddered into life a little before midnight. It moved sluggishly across the tarmac, halted for a moment, then with the roar of some legendary dragon espying its prey lurched forward and soared into the clouds. This was no night for sleep. The sun was circling the earth to meet us. Service of drinks was slow and followed by an ample meal. The first light of dawn was glimmering as our supper-trays were cleared, and breakfast followed almost immediately, though it was hardly a fast which was being broken. We made good time across the Atlantic; it was 6.30 British time when the air hostess came over the loudspeaker: 'Fasten your seatbelts please; we are about to land in Prestwick.' On international flights they repeat announcements in the language of both countries concerned, in this instance American and English. There was no mistake; even my absence of geography sensed something amiss. I said: 'Prestwick? But I'm due for an interview in London at 11.' The stewardess said: 'London's fog-bound. We're landing in Prestwick.'

We landed at Prestwick. We deplaned: or so we were told. Prestwick at 7 a.m. of a Monday morning may not be God-forsaken, but it is assuredly man-forsaken. It wasn't even possible to get a drink of whisky—not that I drink whisky. In the most literal sense we cooled our heels for two hours. At 9 a.m. I managed to get through on the phone with an account of my latitude and longitude. At 9.10 the air hostess came along: 'Will you please replane? We are about to leave for Pay-ris.' I said: 'Paris? But I'm due for an interview in London at 11.' She said: 'Gee, you can get any place from Pay-ris; you can't get any place from here.'

We replaned, and took off into the mists of the morning. But before long we were in brilliant sunshine, and the sun, like Milton's celestial light, began to purge and disperse the mists. We changed course and dropped down to Heathrow after all. It was now about 11 o'clock. Another phone call assured me that though the interviewing committee had dispersed like the mists, it could be reconvened. The airport bus took me to Victoria a short walk to a dignified house in Belgrave Square ('Hearts just as pure and fair May beat in Belgrave Square As in the lowly air Of Seven Dials'—Sullivan's catchy phrases pulsated through my head). I reported and was told to come back for 2.30. I found a delicatessen and bought a pork pie and a yoghourt.

The interviewing committee was in measure a comforting sight. Ritchie Calder had worked with my father in the British Association; I knew him only slightly, but had long admired his internationalism. Michael Stephens, one of the BBC representatives, I had not seen for many years, but had known at school and college. The others turned out to be Stafford of the Department of Education and Science, a very competent and friendly man; John Scupham, also of the BBC; and Walter Perry, the newly appointed Vice-Chancellor of the Open University. I don't remember much about the interview. John Scupham conducted much of it, gentle and kindly, but at the same time searching and incisive. I remember admiring his technique, and seeking to learn from it while suffering from it; he succeeded in being exacting without being frightening. He is the finest and most formidable interviewer I have ever encountered. Ritchie Calder asked whether I thought the materials which the Open University would prepare might be of use to those parts of tropical Africa which I knew. I answered that I thought that the Open University *system* had immense possibilities in the developing countries, but that it was educationally vital that courses should be related to the culture of the students, and that we had too many Nigerians who knew all about English Tudor history and had never heard of Mali or Songhai. Michael Stephens properly did not say much, and I noted that the Vice-Chancellor (as the Greek proverb puts it), having two ears and one tongue, listened more than he spoke. I must have stood up to John Scupham's barrage. They asked me to withdraw, and little more than five minutes later I found myself the first Director of Studies in Arts at the Open University.

The committee dispersed again. I spent an hour chatting over a drink with the Vice-Chancellor about future plans; walked briskly down to Victoria, caught the airport bus, boarded the last plane to New York, and was in bed in Hampton, Virginia, within twenty-four hours of leaving the United States. My appointment to a university which was to use the resources of modern technology had certainly demonstrated those resources.

I come from a scientific family. My father was a physicist of some distinction, my mother the most brilliant botanist of her day in the University of Wales. One uncle was a household-name in plant physiology, another a child-psychologist of some eminence. I had been marked out as a mathematician. But my father, a man of unusual breadth in more senses than one, was eager that I should know some classical Greek. From the first the Greeks held me captive, though I was proud to walk hopefully through the entrance to Plato's Academy beneath the sign 'All hope abandon ye who enter here without knowledge of geometry'. I turned to the classics, and it was the classics which I read at Cambridge. The war supervened on my studies. I spent four years in the London Civil Defence and whiled away the hours of standing-by in taking a theological degree. Then, after a year's school-teaching of miscellaneous subjects, back to Cambridge for Part II, and university posts first at Newcastle upon Tyne and then in London.

My wife and I were much involved with the peace-movement and internationalism through the United Nations Association and Fellowship of Reconciliation. In particular I was continually pressing the needs of the developing countries. A nagging voice inside kept saying 'Talking's all very well, but what are you doing about it?' In 1956 J. T. Saunders, Principal of the then University College, Ibadan, Nigeria, invited me to become their first Professor of Classics. It was a challenge and opportunity too great to miss. We knew that it might be academic suicide, but we burned our boats and had the ten most exciting and rewarding years of our lives. We saw the university through to autonomy; we saw my former students returning to the academic and administrative staff; we saw others going into the schools, into business and industry, into the diplomatic and civil services. We saw the country to independence, and, tragically, to the break-up of the first republic. And we shared in drama and sport and singing and dancing and worship, and in the fascinating search to see that the best of Nigerian traditions and the best of European traditions came together in these activities.

Then, after ten years, the invitation came to go as Hill Visiting Professor of Classics to the University of Minnesota. Here the opportunities were different. A tri-state programme in which Minnesota, Wisconsin and Iowa all shared meant a graduate school of fifty, half a dozen or more of whom will be major classical scholars in fifteen years' time. It seemed right to accept. We had said on appointment to Ibadan that eight to twelve years was the right period; personal and family reasons called us back to Britain when the right opening offered. Once again we burned our boats; this time without even immediate security. We became absorbed with the graduate students, and Minnesota generously offered me a permanent appointment. Unfortunately our visa allowed a maximum stay of four years; but anything beyond two was problematic. In 1968 I was invited to spend a year as first holder of the office of Old Dominion Visiting Professor in Humanities at Hampton Institute, Virginia, a predominantly Black college which was astonishingly celebrating its centennial. Minnesota generously granted me leave of absence. It looked at one time as if permission to return would have to be the subject of a special appendix to a Congressional Bill (this is how it is done in the US: a bill on pollution in the Susquehanna may have as Appendix 14 that John Ferguson be permitted to take a post in Hampton Institute), but the work of the local Congressman and the threat of Senator Abe Ribicoff was sufficient.

The right post in Britain had been obstinately slow in appearing. It had been our experience—which we would understand in theological terms—that the right door opens, but seldom easily or immediately. Then, out of the blue, came a letter from a former Newcastle student, who had been my departmental secretary in Nigeria, and remained (and remains) a close personal friend, enclosing an advertisement for the post of Director of Studies in Arts at the Open University. She wrote: 'This sounds like you.' It did; hence the transatlantic flight.

As this is a personal account, it is worth asking what in the Open University attracted us, and what in my previous career might have led the Open University to offer me an appointment. They are both relevant questions. For our life for twenty years had been absorbed by students. We shared a deep concern about effective teaching, about the right function of lectures, about lecturing in such a way as to stimulate, inform and inspire, about the organization of seminars and tutorials, and drawing out the quieter students, about the helpful direction of the student who is going to be and in some ways is already a finer scholar than you are yourself, and about the aid to the student who is floundering, aid which will make possible for him the elements of basic understanding. We were also much involved in extra-curricular activities together with students, in religious societies and chapel life, in music and drama and poetry, in societies concerned with internationalism and peace, and in sport. I had from time to time been officially engaged in helping students in their corporate and individual life, as Tutor at Newcastle, and as Master of Kuti Hall at Ibadan. We had entertained students regularly in our various homes. Many of our closer friends today are former students. All this would inevitably, as it seemed, go in a system primarily directed to teaching at a distance. Why then make such a change?

Let it be said straight away that the break has not been quite so abrupt. My wife and I do not live in day-to-day contact with students throughout the year. But visits to study centres and day-schools and in particular week-long periods at summer schools do give the chance of serious face-to-face teaching; participation by students in the University Council, General Assembly and other bodies has been another valuable form of contact; and it is surprising how friendships can blossom from such small beginnings. We do not see students in our home as frequently as in the past, but we have not ceased altogether to entertain them. The river has become a stream, but it has not dried up. But this is not the answer, for we did not at first envisage this.

The answer, as we shaped it when we first thought about the post, was threefold. Firstly, if the Open University was doing the job it set out to do, we would be bringing university education to many who, often through no fault of their own, had been deprived of the normal openings, who would by definition never have the opportunity of those face-to-face encounters which we valued so highly, and would have nothing at all but what we could offer them. There was then the responsibility to provide for these education which was intellectually of a reputable university standard, and within the limits of an ineluctably impersonal system to personalize it as strongly as possible.

Secondly, we were both excited about the possibility of pioneering in new methods of education, particularly over the use of radio and TV. I think I had more ideas then than I have now; stern practicalities have intervened! This was exciting in itself, but there was an undercurrent in our thoughts which related directly to personal encounter in education. We knew well, precisely because we were in touch with students, that in the conventional universities many students would pass through their whole student career without any effective personal confrontation with individual members of staff. In Buber's language, there was no I–Thou encounter. General degree students seldom had it at all; honours degree students often missed it unless they were in small and unfashionable departments. In some of the larger American institutions most of the undergraduate teaching was done by Teaching Assistants, and many members of the academic faculty did not meet undergraduates at all. Further, much that goes by the name of teaching in the conventional universities is utterly unworthy of the name. The assumption that teaching is an automatic offshoot of scholarship is only just being challenged. In fact the inadequacy of university teaching has become so notorious that I have heard it seriously said by an appointing committee of one internal candidate for a chair: 'We hear he is a good teacher; he can't be a scholar.' When lectures are inaudible, however learned, they are useless, and the same is true if they are badly organized, or even when they are used to pour out strings of facts which cannot possibly be taken in aurally and which ought to be presented in writing. Now an interesting and important investigation carried out in the University of Minnesota showed that, although students think they get more out of small classes (and psychologically that fact cannot be ignored), they learn more in large classes, and it makes no difference whether those classes are conducted 'live' or through television. When one reflects on the lamentable standard of the closed-circuit television programmes used in the freshman psychology class of 2,000 in that generally admirable institution, it doesn't say much for the lecturing! We had a sneaking suspicion that if the University could develop effective methods for teaching large numbers of students simultaneously at a distance, this could have an impact on the conventional universities in getting rid of wasteful and inefficient teaching and *freeing the members of staff for genuine personal encounters.*

Thirdly. for much of my time as a university teacher, especially in recent years, I had been teaching rather older students. In

Nigeria when we first went the average age of freshmen was somewhere around 26 to 28, and though with developing schools this dropped, there was always a high proportion of older students around. In Minnesota I had been predominantly though not exclusively concerned with graduate students. The Open University was going to provide something new in the form of cooperative teaching. None of us was able at this stage to see how it was going to work out; but we did see that the academic staff were going to be collaborating in a way and to a degree unknown in other universities. We hoped that we would be able to fill the senior posts with men of established reputation and proved ability. We thought from the first that other posts would be likely to go to young men and women, recently graduated, at most with a research degree behind them as well. There were two reasons for this. They were more likely to be open to new methods and approaches before they had become established in other routines. Alongside this, the Open University was something new; it might prove a flop; it was dangerously subject to the ebb and flow of politics. It would be a dedicated man who gave up a secure post elsewhere for one of our lectureships. In fact we were right in this; for a fairly high proportion of our lecturers, this was their first post. But these were very much in the same group as the best of the graduate students in Minnesota, much the same in age and much the same in ability. My task was to do what I could to help them as they found their own style as teachers, as in Minnesota it had been to do what I could to help them to find their own style as scholars, and the opportunities of reading and commenting on drafts of teaching material were not so very different from the opportunities of hearing and commenting on seminar papers. We hoped to establish a similar pattern of mutual intellectual stimulus and personal friendship.

What then had I to offer of interest to the Open University? The answer must be speculative, but the question is pertinent, for it may throw light on some of the differences of approach in those early days. One thing was clear. They were not interested in me as a classicist. There was no intention of developing classics as an academic discipline, and those who bore the responsibility were unlikely to be impressed by the cliché of the general value of a classical education; it could no longer be said of this, in the words of Dean Gaisford, that it 'gave you a sense of superiority over your less fortunate fellow-men and laid open before you positions of considerable emolument both in this world and the world to come'. Nor were they interested in me as a Christian and theologian. I was not in any case a professional theologian, and my contributions were the occasional reflections of an academic on broader or detailed aspects of his faith and its out-working. And the Planning Committee contained a fair number of atheists and agnostics of the older sort, who were more likely to look askance at my Christian activism than to favour it. What was interesting in the appointment was that the very things which made me disreputable in some academic circles must have been actual recommendations. In the first place, I was interested in too many things. Classicists ought not to write on theology, or on Christopher Fry, or on Thomas Young, or on international affairs. Even within the classics they ought to stick to their last, and not be writing at one moment about a pre-Socratic philosopher, at the next about a Greek tragedy, and at the next about a Roman poet. It makes one difficult to classify; the University of London had to invent a category 'Miscellaneous' to describe my publications. But this very breadth meant that I was the more able within the Arts Faculty, and indeed the University as a whole, to take what Plato calls a 'synoptic' view. And indeed my classical training pointed in the same direction. For you cannot go through a real classical education without mastering two very different languages, one refined and precise, the other firm and concrete, and delving in some depth into history, literature and philosophy. If the course is any good you will also have some acquaintance with religion, art history and criticism, and archaeology. Further, although I have expounded this analytically, it is really wrong to do so. You cannot isolate Plato the philosopher from Plato the literary artist, or either from the context of his times. This synoptic approach was vital to the development of the Arts Faculty.

Secondly, I had served abroad. In too many British universities there is a prejudice, the graver because it is wholly unconscious, against applicants from overseas. There is an underlying assumption that no one would go overseas if he could command a post of comparable responsibility—and income—in Britain. The Open University seemed to treat service overseas as evidence of a pioneering spirit. At the very least it was recognized that anyone who had worked in other countries could hardly fail to be enriched by the experience, and would not be hidebound by the conventions of British academic life, but would bring different experiences and insights. It seemed that in the eyes of the Open University selectors, experience overseas was a plus in the accounts. The Vice-Chancellor himself had worked for a period in West Africa, the University Secretary had been in government service in East Africa, the Finance Officer had been in Northern Nigeria, and other senior administrators included one appointed from government service in Fiji, another from the West African Examinations Council, and yet another who was himself a West Indian. Of the original four deans, two were appointed from posts overseas, as was one of the other two subsequent appointments. When the appointments of professors and other senior academics came round, of the five professors in the Arts Faculty, one was at Dar-es-Salaam, one in Vancouver, and a third American-born, and the sub-dean (a later appointment) came from Rhodesia; the senior social scientists included men working in Australia, Nigeria and Rhodesia; the professor of chemistry came from the University of the West Indies. Something of the same spirit permeated through in the selection of secretaries and typists. One of the first senior appointments in this field was a woman with long experience as a secretary in Nigeria, and one readily thinks of others who have lived and worked in other parts of Africa and of the world. They may be well-disposed towards the University as a prospective employer, but the University is well-disposed towards them as prospective employees.

Thirdly, I had been a head of department for ten years, and twice Dean of the Faculty of Arts during that period. I had acquired a deal of administrative experience, and, equally important, learned to carry it lightly. In addition I had been involved with public affairs from an early stage. At Cambridge I had been secretary and later chairman of a number of university societies; I had been chairman of a national organization at the age of thirty-two. I knew something of committees and their ways. I had seen the skill of politicians in manipulating committee-procedure to their own ends. I had also seen, admired and tried to share in the Quaker approach of finding 'the sense of the meeting'. To this we must return. Meantime, enough to note that this public experience and open approach seemed acceptable to the authorities. It was clear that we were going to be a small, closely knit team; it was important to foster the sense of responsible participation in a communal activity, to develop, in fact, what it is fashionable to call 'group dynamics'. And though I had never called it that, I had a good deal of experience in the field.

Fourthly, I had been primarily a teacher. I had made my contributions to the advancement of learning; one could hardly be an effective university teacher unless one's mind was continually playing around the subjects one was discussing with students and seeking fresh insights about them. But in so far as I had a reputation at all, it was as a teacher rather than as a scholar. I had taken pains to make myself as good a lecturer as possible. I had tried, in communicating, always to be alert to students, to be conscious of them, their interests and concerns. I had done an edition of the tenth book of Plato's *Republic* in which I was trying to relate students' reading and understanding of Plato to their other reading and thinking. These are values which are largely unrecognized by other university appointment committees. A man can be as dull as ditchwater and get his chair, provided that the weight of his articles tips the scales against other candidates. I have not known a man awarded a chair because of the brilliance of his teaching. There would be little room in the Open University for the manifestation of the more obvious teaching skills which I had developed; but the committee may have thought that a man whose chief concern had been communication would have some use in developing new forms and patterns of communication.

So the Open University showed itself from the first, without (I hope) in any way lessening the properly stringent academic requirements for a university appointment, open to less obvious and less fashionable values.

CHAPTER TWO

A Historical Sketch

In an American radio magazine in 1922 appeared the words 'The people's University of the Air will have a greater student body than all our universities put together' (Tunstall 178). In 1926 in England, J. C. Stobart, author of two reliable pieces of higher popular education, *The Glory that was Greece* and *The Grandeur that was Rome*, mooted something similar (Tunstall 113). The time was not ripe.

In 1963 two events took place of some importance to the emergence of the Open University. One was the publication of the Robbins Report on Higher Education, the report of the committee, appointed in 1961 under the chairmanship of Lord Robbins 'to review the pattern of full-time higher education in Great Britain and in the light of national needs and resources to advise Her Majesty's Government on what principles its long-term development should be based. In particular, to advise, in the light of these principles, whether there should be any changes in that pattern, whether any new types of institution are desirable and whether any modifications should be made in the present arrangements for planning and coordinating the development of the various types of institution'.

The Robbins Committee, concerned as it was with full-time higher education, did not come up with any firm recommendations for an institution such as the Open University. But they did (§821) speak of the potential value of 'the establishment by some universities of correspondence courses'. They thought that the numbers should be restricted so that personal contact could be maintained, that there should be intensive direct teaching during the normal university summer vacation, and that television as a technique of educational communication would have considerable potential value as an ancillary. Only in the Soviet Union did they find anything of this kind systematically applied, and they commented (§114) that 'whatever might be thought elsewhere they themselves believe that this method of study is of considerable value in itself, since it does not segregate students from the general social and economic life of the country'.

These *obiter dicta* did not attract much attention at the time. The general impact of the report was to leave the sense that Britain stood with the Soviet Union in opposition to the rest of the Western world in the high selectivity of its university entrance policy, and that there was need for a massive expansion of provision for higher education. Thus in Britain 4.5 per cent of the appropriate age-group entered full-time degree or degree-level courses, compared with 7 per cent in France, 10 per cent in Sweden and 20 per cent in the US (§123), though the figure is somewhat misleading as much of the work done in universities in the US is done in sixth forms in Britain. The Committee recommended across twenty years an increase in full-time university places in Great Britain from 130,000 to 346,000, and in all full-time higher education from 216,000 to 558,000 (§494). But more important ultimately than these figures was the clear evidence, spelt out in the volume of appendices, of very large 'reserves of untapped ability'. They showed, for example, that children whose fathers were in the higher professional group were eleven times as likely to enter full-time higher education as children of skilled manual workers, and twenty-two times as likely as children of unskilled manual workers (the discrepancy for girls being even more alarming); children whose fathers continued their education to the age of eighteen were eight times as likely to enter full-time higher education as those whose fathers left school before the age of sixteen; and that, of those who had the opportunity of staying on till eighteen, the percentage of those achieving two A-level examination passes was not significantly different between those whose fathers were in the higher professional group and those whose fathers were skilled manual workers (§§137-46). In other words, the evidence pointed to the fact that substantial numbers of people capable of succeeding in higher education were not having the opportunity of showing what they could do. It was this, established as it was by the careful accumulation of evidence, which directed the way to the Open University. For if Robbins directed a challenge to the present and future, there was a larger challenge in catching up with the past.

The other event of 1963 was the succession of Harold Wilson to the leadership of the Labour Party. At the time of Hugh Gaitskell's untimely death Wilson was on a speaking-tour of the United States. While he was there he gave a good deal of thought to the question of higher education. He had been impressed by a suggestion, which had originated with Professor (later Sir) George Catlin in 1946, been revised by Professor George Wedell in 1961, and emanated in a really effective form from Michael Young, an educational thinker of some originality, who had sketched the possibility of a television university. The Crowther study of ex-service personnel in 1959 had shown large numbers with high intelligence who had left school at sixteen. Wilson saw that in the United States a much higher proportion of eighteen-year-olds have the opportunity of higher education. At the same time the drop-out rate in the freshman year is fantastically large, rising to about 50 per cent. This is a waste of everyone's time. It is a waste for those who are not responding to full-time university education, and a waste for those who teach them. It is a major factor in the almost total withdrawal, in some universities, of the established academic staff from freshman teaching, and sometimes from undergraduate teaching. Wilson knew well the Soviet use of radio and correspondence courses for degree teaching. At the same time he saw the immense potential of television in every home, and the lamentable failure to use this opportunity for constructive purposes. He was friendly with Senator Benton, and admired the Encyclopaedia Britannica's development of educational films. He conceived a vision in which television would be used to bring higher education into every home in the land—a home-based television university.

Wilson outlined his scheme for a University of the Air in a campaign speech in Glasgow in 1963, and for better or for worse the University of the Air became a minor issue in the general election of 1964; this meant that it was being taken seriously, but it had the unfortunate effect of setting one or two Conservatives, notably Iain Macleod, rigorously and almost fanatically against it. When Labour came to power, Wilson handed over responsibility for realizing his dream to Jennie Lee, later Baroness Lee of Asheridge, who was at the time Under-Secretary of State for Education and Science. Jennie Lee played a notable part in bringing the Open University to birth: she was adamant that it should not be 'Paddy, the next best thing'; hence its familiar characterization as 'by Harold Wilson out of Jennie Lee'. Edward Short, not a man to indulge his emotions, was reported at the point when the Labour government went out of office, to have put his arm round her shoulders and said: 'Jennie, the great achievement of the first post-war Labour administration was the National Health Service, and that was Nye's. The great achievement of the second is the Open University, and that's yours.' The result of Jennie Lee's determination was the establishment of a Parliamentary Committee which in February 1966 produced the White Paper *A University of the Air*. Even with the White Paper, the University was no more than a vaguely outlined sketch; it was clear that much hard preliminary planning was needed if it was ever to get off the ground and really into the air.

Accordingly, after Parliamentary debate, in September 1967 the Secretary of State established a Planning Committee under the chairmanship of Sir Peter Venables, Vice-Chancellor of the University of Aston in Birmingham. Peter Venables is a wise and experienced academic statesman, as well as being a chairman of remarkable skill in the swift transaction of important business without inhibiting discussion. He agreed to accept the chairmanship on one condition—that there were no politicians on the Planning Committee. The result was, or ought to have been, to take the University altogether out of the field of polemical party politics. The Planning Committee was in fact as weighty a body of educationists as you could hope to draw together. It comprised the Vice-Chancellors of Aston, Cambridge, Exeter, Hull and Sussex, as well as a former Vice-Chancellor of Sussex, the Warden of Coleg Harlech and the Principal of Lancaster College of Technology, four Professors, representatives of educational broadcasting both from the BBC and the Independent Television Authority, the Director of the University of Glasgow Television Service, the Director of the Centre for Educational Technology at the University of Sussex, the General Secretary of the Association of Education Committees, the Deputy Education Officer of the Inner London Education Authority, and the Chairman of the Arts Council. It was in fact a rather weightier body than the Robbins Commission. The initial scepticism on the part of the other universities about the Open University showed no great confidence in their own best representatives.

The full committee met ten times, and its three working groups, on Ways and Means, Students and Curriculum, and Constitution and Organization, met on a further forty-one occasions. The committee used surveys and other techniques to suggest that the potential student body might lie between 170,000 and 450,000, and that those with the immediate intention of registering as students would be not less than 34,000 and not more than about 150,000. These estimates have proved very accurate. Their figures suggest also that the Open University would not be meeting an immediate emergency so much as fulfilling a continuing need and continuing demand. They felt that those aged sixteen to twenty-one should study through sandwich courses, block release or day release, and that the Open University should serve the adult student, and drew on the experience of the University of New England, Armidale, New South Wales, to show that adult students can successfully take a university degree by a system primarily dependent on correspondence. They further saw the potentiality of the Open University for post-experience courses, updating those already working in a particular field, or enabling them to grasp what is happening in fields other than their own.

The major change from Wilson's original vision was the realization that it was not possible for the University to rely solely or even primarily on broadcasting: 'It is . . . neither practically possible nor pedagogically sound to rely on broadcasting as the principal or exclusive means of instruction in an operation designed to provide disciplined courses of university level.' Broadcasting would have a significant role in association with other means of instruction. This was based on common sense; it was also based on experience from Japan, from the Munich *Telekolleg*, from the Chicago City Junior College, from Wellington in New Zealand, from New South Wales, from Radio Sorbonne, from a Polish scheme supported by UNESCO, and from the British National Extension College.

The Planning Committee, guided in this by Norman Mackenzie, decided from the first that in the British universities degree structures were too rigid and too specialized. The courses offered should approximate more to the familar 'general' degree, rather than being confined to any particular specialisms, though there should be specialist courses among those available. At the same time they did not want the excessive fragmentation of the

American degree. In the British universities, students who embark upon a degree programme may find that they have little or no choice left them, perhaps no more than to opt for mathematics or physics for their subsidiary or to choose between Vergil and Horace for their special author. In America a typical degree programme involves the accumulation of 180 credits, one credit representing the successful completion of a course involving one lecture or seminar each week for a term, and steady progress involving about fifteen credits a term or forty-five in an academic year. The choice is circumscribed in some ways: freshman English may be compulsory, arts students may have to take a course in laboratory science, and graduate schools may demand a particular 'mix'. But it is a frequent occurrence that students are desperately trying to find some course which will bring them in three more credits. The Planning Committee offered a solution which combines the freedom of the American system with the general sense of direction existing in the British system. They proposed a credit-system; but graduation would be on six credits, and honours would be awarded on eight credits. A credit thus represented the successful achievement of a course which would last a full academic year and have as its academic content approximately half a normal university year's work. They also proposed that students should take two 'foundation courses' before proceeding further, and that four should be initially offered, Mathematics, Understanding Science, Literature and Culture, and Understanding Society. 'The initial challenge that faces the academic staff is so to devise these courses that the whole of a broad field is explored in a way that will stimulate and excite students with very varied backgrounds; but that will, at the same time, make intellectual demands upon them of the same order as the demands made by any normal first-year university course.' These 'lines' would each lead to about four component fields of study; mathematics might lead to statistics, or computer science, or pure mathematics and so on. This scheme offered students considerable flexibility of choice without hopeless fragmentation. They could proceed through the system at their own pace, though they should not take more than two credits in any one year.

The concept has stood the test of experience well. The proposed course on Literature and Culture ended up as *Humanities: An Introduction*. The 'lines' have become faculties. Additional faculties have been established in Technology, which offers a foundation course, and Education, which does not. Students are not required to take both their foundation courses before proceeding further. One other change is the innovation of the half-credit course at later levels. Two credits in a year was a severe strain on all but the hardiest; one a year seemed a snail's progress. The half-credit offered a compromise.

The Planning Committee decided, on a proposal from Roderick MacLean of the University of Glasgow Television Service, on an academic year which ran from January to December. They envisaged courses running for forty teaching weeks, with a break in the summer for short-term residential courses using accommodation in other universities available only at that period. This would also mean that examinations would be held in November and December at the 'off-peak' time for other examinations. For operational reasons the forty weeks was reduced initially to 36 and subsequently to 34 and then 32. The difference of academic year is a handicap in pioneering joint courses with other institutions, but the practical judgement has on the whole been upheld. Curiously, the Planning Committee did not state in print the number of hours a week which a student might be expected to work. In fact they arrived at a notional figure of ten hours a week for a single course. This, with an intensive week's summer school and a period of revision and examination, gave a reasonable equivalent to half a normal university year's work. Most students put in more hours than that, and with the shortening of the courses it was expected that students would put in eleven to twelve hours a week.

The Committee decided initially to contract the BBC to provide the production and transmission services for the University. The BBC agreed to provide thirty hours a week for television and thirty hours for radio, and agreed to the Open University having its TV programmes between 5.30 and 7.30 on weekday evenings, and during the day at weekends. The nature of the relationship with the BBC is important. People used to speak loosely of 'the BBC University', and I have heard a senior Conservative politician explain the initial hostility of his party to the Open University as arising from 'suspicion of those left-wingers in the BBC'. Officially, the University is completely independent of the BBC, and simply employs the BBC to do a job. In actual working, however, there is a genuine sense of partnership, not least at the grassroots.

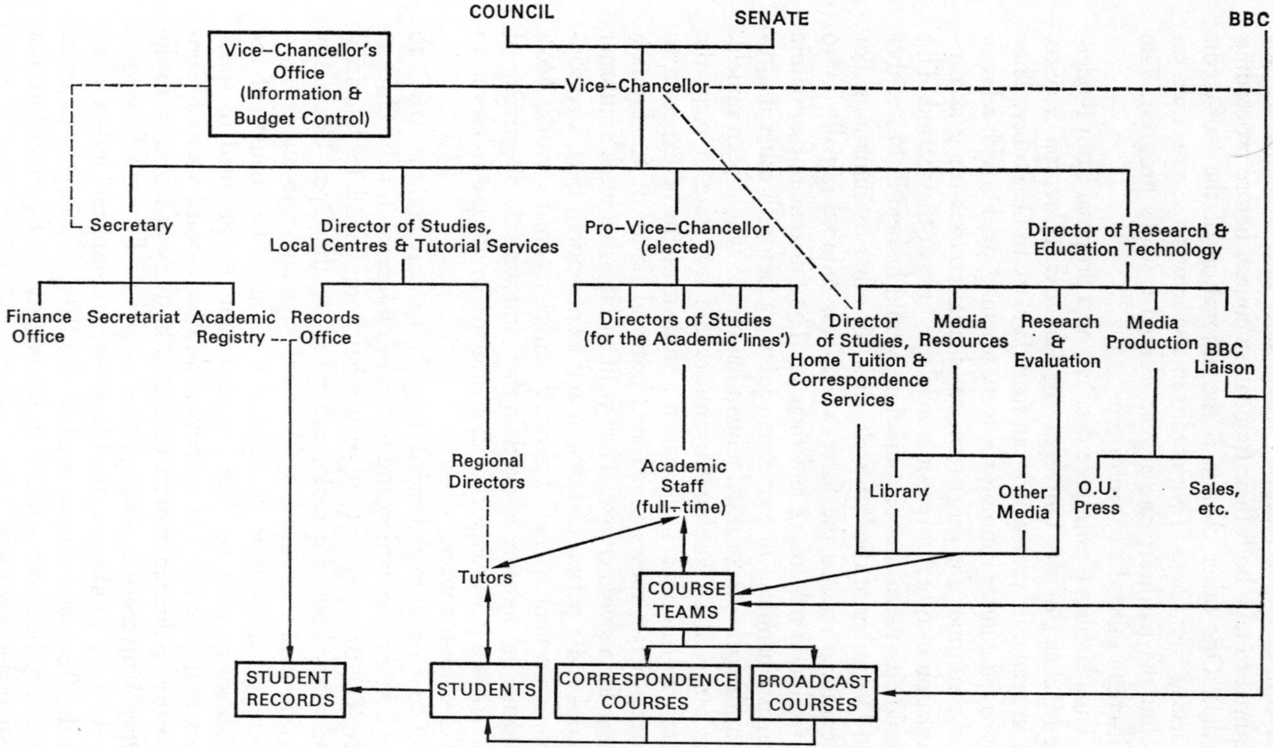

FIG. 1 The structure as envisaged by the Planning Committee

The Committee also gave the University its governmental structure, and in 1968, before presenting its report, made two initial appointments of great importance. Professor Walter Perry, who was at the time Vice-Principal of the University of Edinburgh, became the first Vice-Chancellor, and Anastasios Christodoulou, Deputy Secretary of the University of Leeds, was appointed University Secretary. The structure proposed is shown in the accompanying diagram (fig. 1). Some of the nomenclature has changed, but the structure on the left and in the centre of the diagram has for the most part stood the test, though that on the right has undergone considerable changes in the light of experience.

The Vice-Chancellor and Secretary came into post officially on 1 January 1969. In the early months of the year a Royal Charter was drawn up for the University, and received the Royal Assent on 30 May. The Charter was ceremonially presented by Sir Godfrey Agnew, Clerk of the Privy Council, in the rooms of the Royal Society on 23 July 1969. At the ceremony Lord Crowther was inducted as the first Chancellor. Geoffrey Crowther was a remarkable man, a man of vision and integrity. His most famous work was done through *The Economist*, and his contribution to the Crowther Report made him an outstandingly appropriate choice. His integrity suffered severe strains in the business world, and the collapse of his work with Trust Houses shortened his life tragically; he died early in 1972. Even during the brief period that remained he was no figurehead Chancellor, but active in enthusiasm and wise in guidance. He was no orator in the grand manner; yet I remember him swaying the most unexpected people by his peroration in the Cambridge Union just after the war. For the inaugural ceremony he had three speeches to make, one in the afternoon and two at a banquet on the same evening; each was precisely fitted to the moment. His address at the Royal Society has remained one of the most memorable formulations of what the Open University is about:

> We are open, first, as to *people*. Not for us the carefully regulated escalation from one educational level to the next by which the traditional universities establish their criteria for admission.
>
> The first, and most urgent, task before us is to cater for the many thousands of people, fully capable of a higher education, who, for one reason or another, do not get it, or do not get as much of it as

they can turn to advantage, or as they discover, sometimes too late, that they need. Only in recent years have we come to realize how many such people there are, and how large are the gaps in educational provision through which they can fall. The existing system, for all its expansion, misses and leaves aside a great unused reservoir of human talent and potential. Men and women drop out through failures in the system, through disadvantages of their environment, through mistakes of their own judgment, through sheer bad luck. These are our primary material. To them we offer a further opportunity.

But if this were all, we could hardly call ourselves a University. This is not simply an educational rescue mission—though that is our first task, and we do not decry it. But we also aim wider and higher. Wherever there is an unprovided need for higher education, supplementing the existing provision, there is our constituency. . . .

The Open University is not the rival of the existing universities. It is designed to take over where they are compelled to leave off. . . .

We are open as to *places*. This University has no cloisters—a word meaning closed. Hardly even shall we have a campus. By a very happy chance, our only local habitation will be in the new city that is to bear two of the widest-ranging names in the history of English thought, Milton Keynes. But this is only where the tip of our toe touches ground. The rest of the University will be disembodied and airborne. From the start, it will flow all over the United Kingdom. . . .

We are open as to *methods*. We start, in dependence on, and in grateful partnership with, the BBC. But already the development of technology is marching on, and I predict that before long actual broadcasting will form only a small part of the University's output. The world is caught in a Communications Revolution . . . Every new form of human communication will be examined to see how it can be used to raise and broaden the level of human understanding. . . .

We are open, finally, to *ideas*. It has been said that there are two aspects of education, both necessary. One regards the individual human mind as a vessel of varying capacity, into which is to be poured as much as it will hold of the knowledge and experience by which human Society lives and moves. This is the Martha of education—and we shall have plenty of these tasks to perform. But the Mary regards the human mind more as a fire that has to be set alight and blown with the divine efflatus. That also we take as our ambition. . . .

Sir Peter Venables was the obvious choice as Pro-Chancellor and Chairman of the University Council. The University found an outstanding Treasurer in Sir Paul Chambers, a man of enormous experience in the world of finance, whose active concern for education was soon to be further recognized by his appointment as Pro-Chancellor of the University of Kent. The Council numbered a maximum of thirty-nine; it included six members of the Planning Committee in addition to Venables, six members of the Senate, and representatives of those areas of public life, such as the local education authorities, likely to be most intimately concerned with the University. It thus combined those intimately engaged with the work of the University with others who could take a more detached view, and among these last those engaged in higher education elsewhere with others representing the general public and what one might call consumer interests. The Council is large enough to offer a spread of experience and wisdom, but not so large as to be unwieldy.

Alongside the Council, the Charter established an Academic Advisory Committee charged with 'keeping under review the standard of the education provided in the University and of the degrees awarded by the University'. This is a comparatively small body of eight academics from other institutions, together with the Vice-Chancellor, meeting under the chairmanship of Professor Hilde Himmelweit of the London School of Economics. It might be said that they bear the same relation to the general academic development of the University that external examiners bear to academic awards, except that their function is a strictly advisory one. They form a valuable 'House of Lords' in referring back matters of academic policy whose full implications may not have been realized, and although their function is advisory it would be rash of any faculty or board to reject their advice without cogent reasons.

An early decision had to be taken about the siting of the University. We were able to operate temporarily from premises in Belgrave Square. This was all right for a short period when the numbers of central staff were small, and the operations in an embryonic stage, but it could not possibly cope with even the initial full-scale preparations. Central London was out of the question: property was too expensive and there was no room for expansion. At the same time there were two cardinal reasons for being in range of London. One was that a national organization is most appropriately sited within reach of the capital; its external committees must be nationally representative, and it could expect (and has received) large numbers of overseas visitors. The other arose out of the partnership with the BBC. Programmes would be made at Alexandra Palace; it was essential that the academics concerned with those programmes should be able to travel easily to Alexandra Palace, and that London-based BBC staff should have ready access to the University headquarters. We therefore looked for a site about fifty miles from London, outside the over-crowded commuter belt but inside the possibilities of commutation, and preferably (because of Alexandra Palace) to the north or north-west. A country house had much to commend it. Country houses were on the market. They offered a building for immediate occupation and grounds in which expansion was possible, often in charming surroundings. A number of sites were considered. One was near Didcot; another was Cliveden, the Astors' old house, which would have had piquant political associations for some of us who had sung 'In Bucks there is a country house' to the tune of 'There is a tavern in the town'. In March 1969 the choice lighted on Walton Hall. In itself it is not a building of great distinction, a rambling eighteenth-century brick construction. But it has a really noble front and entrance-block dating from the early nineteenth century, which offers distinguished accommodation for the reception area and offices of the Vice-Chancellor and Secretary. The grounds extend over some seventy acres, including some magnificent cedars of Lebanon which are said to be among the first brought to this country. Communications to London are excellent: Walton is four miles from Bletchley station, which is less than an hour from the London terminus at Euston, and three miles from the nearest access point on the M1 motorway. Communications locally were less satisfactory, and the University had to provide special transport for secretaries and other employees. But in addition to the other advantages of the site it stands within a mile of the centre of the proposed new city of Milton Keynes, which is expected to expand to a quarter of a million people. The Milton Keynes Development Corporation welcomed the association with the Open University. Members of the University felt that in our otherwise somewhat rootless existence there might be something to be said for serving as a cultural and intellectual centre for a whole new city. And Lord Crowther made a point of the siting of the University in a city which bore the names of two of the great figures in British intellectual and cultural history. One might add that, if the University ever wanted to develop a second site, it should be at Newton Purcell! It seems possible that the Corporation may be able to develop a higher education campus around Walton Hall, with the consequent interaction and sharing of facilities.

The architects chosen were Fry, Drew and Partners; they were appointed at the end of February 1969. For me it was the renewal of an old acquaintance, since they had been for some years architects to the University of Ibadan, where their buildings had done much to establish new standards in tropical architecture. Here they showed a similar capacity for good-looking design with a marked sense of linear horizontal movement even for quite tall buildings. Most astonishing, although designing could only begin in March, the first building, an extensive faculty block with two wings, was actually completed and occupied by October. The glorious summer weather helped, but it was a remarkable feat. It was not for nothing that Jane Drew was awarded an honorary degree at the first graduation ceremony. These first buildings were officially opened on 18 May 1970, by Lord Mountbatten who took the opportunity to make a characteristically forthright speech.

Development was by no means confined to the Milton Keynes campus. The Planning Committee had rightly envisaged the need for a regional organization as the basis of the actual teaching. Among the early appointments was that of the Director of Regional Tutorial Services. The country was divided initially into twelve regions: London; South (with headquarters in Oxford); South West (Bristol); West Midlands (Birmingham); East Midlands (Nottingham); East Anglia (Cambridge); Yorkshire (Leeds); North West (Manchester); North East (Newcastle upon Tyne); Wales (Cardiff); Scotland (Edinburgh). The twelfth, Northern Ireland (Belfast), was for the moment under the wing of the North West. Later, the North East changed its name and nature to cover the North from east to west, and a thirteenth region was formed in the South East (East Grinstead). Each of these regions had its own Regional Director. They were responsible for the setting up of study centres in the main centres of population, rooms hired for the purpose perhaps from a Technical College or Teachers' Centre, where students could meet

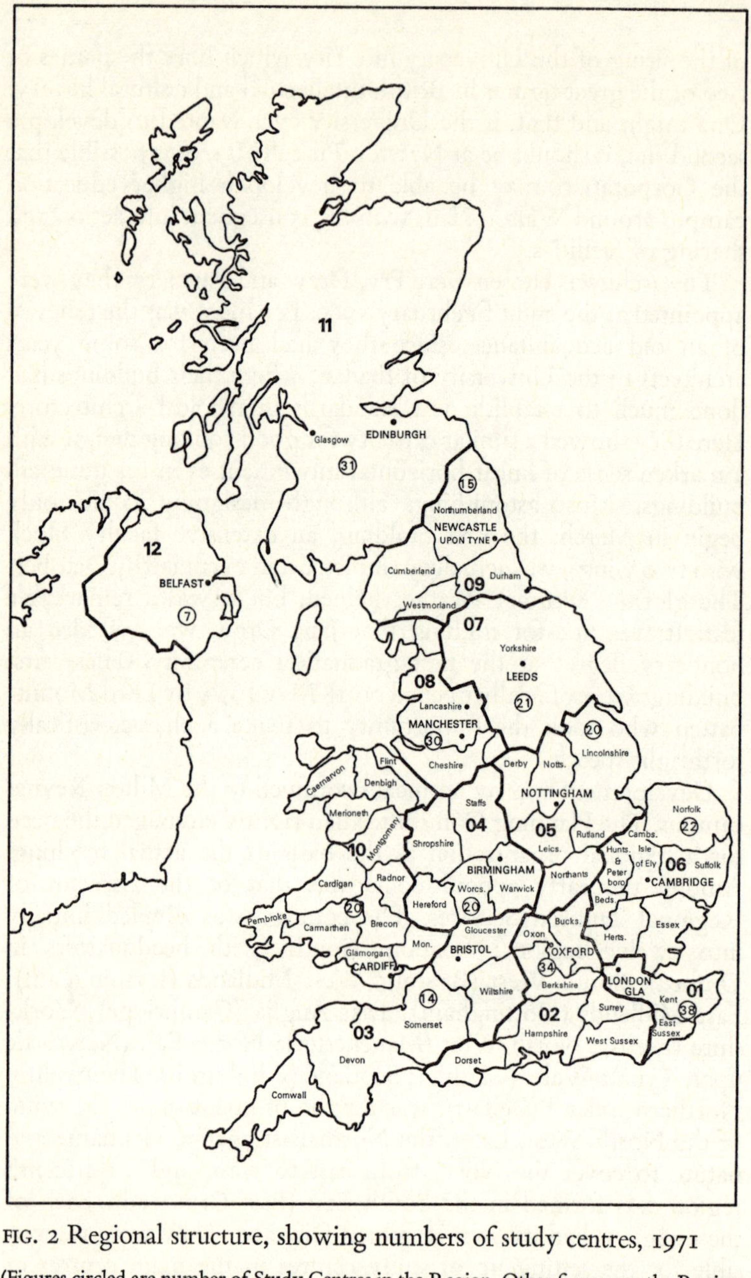

FIG. 2 Regional structure, showing numbers of study centres, 1971

(Figures circled are number of Study Centres in the Region. Other figures are the Region code numbers as follows: 1 London; 2 South; 3 South West; 4 West Midlands; 5 East Midlands; 6 East Anglia; 7 Yorkshire; 8 North West; 9 North; 10 Wales; 11 Scotland; 12 Northern Ireland.)

with one another and with staff, watch and listen to programmes, and which would, it was hoped, develop a corporate life of their own. A rough and ready guide was that a study centre should have within accessible distance eighty or more students, and by the beginning of 1971, 237 of these had been set up. In addition there were thirty-six support centres in remote areas with fewer students; these might be little more than a room to meet in. The Regions were responsible for the whole of the tutorial and counselling operation, a mammoth work whose scale the University is only now beginning to realize.

Initial recruitment of academic staff was at the rate of four per 'discipline' (e.g. history, chemistry, economics). The amount of work involved in the preparation and maintenance of courses of a quite new kind was greatly underestimated, but numbers have not markedly increased. Indeed, it was fondly assumed that the same group of people would take one year over the preparation of the foundation course, one year over the preparation of second-level courses (though there would be three of them), one year over the preparation of third-level courses (though there would be four of them), and would then be ready to remake the foundation course! Today it seems laughable. The first group appointed were in post in the second half of 1969. The decision was taken to admit the first students in January 1971. We knew that we could do with a more leisured run-in. But expectations had been aroused, and undue delay would be frustrating for students and stultifying for us. Better to be presented with an exacting challenge, even if we fulfilled it imperfectly, than to disappoint these expectations.

There was another reason for pressing on. For all Venables's statesmanlike care, the Open University was associated in the minds of many with the Labour Party, and some Conservative leaders had made surprisingly intemperate pronouncements about it. The political situation in 1969 was nicely balanced, and the Conservative victory of 1970 was already a clear prophecy. Unless the University was securely established, there was a distinct possibility that it might be disestablished. Iain Macleod, one of the ablest Conservatives, had declared publicly that if the thing were set up, his party would abolish it. It was at all times difficult to see how the Conservative party of all parties could annul an institution set up by Royal Charter, but the threat was there and with it uncertainty. There is no doubt that Macleod's sudden death, lamentable for national leadership in other ways, eased the University's infancy. In actual fact there were no major problems. Margaret Thatcher, a formidable opponent of the things in which she disbelieves, but an equally strong champion when convinced, as Secretary of State for Education spent a gratifying amount of time in finding out about the Open University. No doubt she sailed in to the attack; it is one of her favourite techniques. Equally, she respects those who stand up to her, and is open to reasonable argument. She emerged from the encounter ready to give the University her support, and was subsequently our main advocate in that government. William van Straubenzee, as Under Secretary, showed himself open. Norman St John Stevas, his successor, had from the first been a supporter. The University was given its chance. If it had failed it would have had no defences against abolition. But it did not fail, and is now unlikely ever to be the shuttlecock of the political parties.

The University decided to admit 25,000 students in January 1971. It was assumed that 5,000 of these would not in any real sense take up the places offered to them, so that there would be an effective student body of 20,000. This assumption was close to the mark. 24,220 students were provisionally registered; 19,581 completed their registration at the end of April. This last figure was the baseline for all subsequent calculations. The withdrawals were heavier in the science-based areas (Mathematics 31.8 per cent, Science 25.2 per cent, Social Science 22.1 per cent, Arts 19.3 per cent) and among the skilled manual workers. The University was greatly hampered at the outset by a national postal strike lasting seven weeks. It is hard to think of many things better suited to upset the work of a new University so dependent on correspondence! The situation, as the Vice-Chancellor put it, 'evoked a Dunkirk spirit'. There was energetic improvisation. Academic and administrative staff buckled to the task of packing up materials, which were despatched to regional centres by road; regional staff distributed them round the study centres; students collected them in person. But there was an alarming backlog. Students were patient and understanding, and their patience and understanding covered some deficiencies for which the postal strike was not responsible: so much so that when the start of the second year's operations was disrupted by an industrial dispute in the power industry, a cynic was heard to comment 'We'll have no excuses left for next year!' More seriously, however, it was a remarkable achievement to overcome these disheartening difficulties at the start. No one had any real idea what proportion of students would successfully complete the first year. Certainly no one would have been surprised if it had been of the order of 50 per cent; after all, that is the figure for many American universities using face-to-face methods. I do not think we would have been surprised, though we would indubitably have been disappointed, if the pass-rate had been 25 per cent. I doubt if anyone expected that credits would be gained by 75.3 per cent of those students who completed their registration. The Vice-Chancellor described it, in a phrase quoted by half the press of Britain, as a 'staggering' success. When we reflect that a significant proportion of the remainder may have been forced to put aside their studies by their own illness, illness in the family, transfer abroad, new responsibility at work or other similar factors, the achievement is remarkable. From that moment the success of the University was assured.

The number of students the University can take depends on government decisions, since the direct cost of any student to the University is not fully covered by his fees. The government decided that the student-body should reach a plateau of 52,000. In the end it was decided to reach this plateau by making 20,000 offers in 1972, 17,000 in 1973, and 15,000 in 1974.

One major controversy confronted the University during its first year of operation. The Planning Committee had seen the University as designed for the over-21s, for those who had missed their normal chance of university education. But there was a national problem in the fact that those eighteen-year-olds qualified for university education greatly exceeded the number of places available. No government of whatever party, out of all the conflicting claims on the budget, could possibly justify all the expenditure needed to provide places for all those qualified for face-to-face residential universities. Had the Open University a part to play in this? The question was discreetly and indirectly asked; there have been no direct pressures from government. But the question was ineluctable and had to be answered. Opinion in the University was divided. Some felt that the University should in no circumstances take eighteen-year-olds, and particularly qualified eighteen-year-olds. The system was designed for mature students in full employment; the idea of finding places for qualified eighteen-year-olds was opposed to the principle of open entry; the University could not and should not become the sixth choice on everyone's UCCA (Universities Central Council on Admissions) form; the admission of eighteen-year-olds in large numbers would change the character of the University, it would inhibit the older disadvantaged students, it might detract from the serious dedicated spirit of application; this was the beginning of a new élitism in higher education, with 'real' university education for the few, and a second best for the many. Others recognized that there was a real problem and thought that the University should at least explore the possibility of helping. Everyone was unanimous in two things, in regretting that the pressure had come before the University had had a chance to find its feet, and in asserting that nothing must detract from the University's true function, and that eighteen-year-olds, if taken at all, must be additional to the normal quota, and funded additionally. What emerged was a typical compromise. The University agreed to admit 500 eighteen-year-olds in each of 1974 and 1975 as a pilot experiment. At the same time it undertook to explore the possibility of joint courses with other institutions of higher education: Milton Keynes College of Education was one such, where proximity made collaboration easy. In actual fact it now seems that the national problem is less severe than originally appeared, and many departments in other universities have not been able to find their full complement of students. It may well be that the Open University's contribution to the solution of the problem will be precisely along the lines of its original foundation. Some of those who at present are choosing not to apply for university courses will later seek university education. They will find the Open University there to offer it.

The credit exemption system, which I shall explain later, meant that some students graduated at the end of 1972. The first graduation ceremony was therefore held in 1973. In the meantime Crowther had died. No man is indispensable, but it was not easy to think of the right replacement. The choice rested on the former Lord Chancellor, Lord Gardiner, and it could not have been a happier one. His wisdom and integrity were admired by those of all parties; his concern for the underprivileged was well known; and he was a vocal supporter of the Open University. The opportunity was taken for a single ceremony combining the installation of the Chancellor, the award of the first honorary degrees, and the first graduation ceremony. It was a singularly impressive occasion. Some of the more radical members of the

University were opposed to ceremonial of any kind, but if there was to be ceremonial, this could hardly have been more fitting or more dignified, and even some of the more hard-headed were not unmoved. It had originally been intended to hold the ceremony at Walton Hall, but this was an aberration, as there was no appropriate accommodation, and it was held instead in the Great Hall of Alexandra Palace. The whole ceremony, organized by Peter Thornton-Pett, a member of the administrative staff who himself had only lately graduated as a mature student from Warwick University after nearly thirty years in the Royal Air Force, went through with perfect timing and without visible hitch. It was televised and seen directly in hundreds of thousands of homes. Music was provided by a bass ensemble, and by Gerald Hendrie, the Professor of Music, on a special electronic organ; the changing of the stops was computerized, the snag being that, if the mainswitch had been turned off for even ten seconds, the performance would have been upset! Honorary degrees were fittingly given to a number of those who, of eminence in their own right, had made notable contributions to the emergence of the University: the new Chancellor; Jennie Lee, who was understandably moved by the occasion; Venables; Lord Hill and Sir Hugh Greene, who had initiated the cooperation with the BBC; Michael Young of the National Extension College, who had early adumbrated the idea of a University of the Air; Jane Drew, the architect; Richard Hoggart, himself a self-made scholar who had come up the hard way, and who had been helpful to the University on selection committees and in other ways; Lord Campbell of the Milton Keynes Development Corporation. It was right too that among the honorary graduates was one who had had no direct association with the University, but whose contribution to the education of the underprivileged was known all over the world. This was Paolo Freire, the Latin American educationist, author of *Pedagogy of the Oppressed.* For Paolo Freire, education is liberation; and these views had led him to prison in his own country; Walter James, in presenting him, commented on the irony that a former Lord Chancellor was investing with a degree a man who had served a term in prison!

After the honorary degrees came the graduation ceremony. The students were presented region by region to the Chancellor by their Regional Directors. Each came out of the body of the hall, bowed to the Chancellor, and took his seat on the platform.

It was an impressive sight for those on the platform to see vast spaces opening up within the body of the hall, and for those in the hall to see the seats stretching far back around the organ filling up with blue-gowned figures—and to realize that these 600-odd who appeared in person, or even the 867 who had completed their degree, were but a drop in the stream of those who were to come in future years. Eventually the platform was full. The Vice-Chancellor spoke briefly and appropriately to the new graduates, reminding them that the currency of the Open University degree would be judged in terms of their work. The congregation was closed. The whole platform party, officers of the University, members of Council, honorary graduates, and all the ordinary graduates, processed out. It was a stroke of genius to trumpet them out to Copland's *Fanfare for the Common Man*.

CHAPTER THREE

Developing the Staff

It may seem topsy-turvy to start from the staff. Yet this effectively is where we had to start, and one of the results is that we have ever since been cutting our coat according to our tailors. For if you have, as we have, a severely limited central academic staff, your lines of development are channelled into their expertise and their enthusiasms.

The first appointment was the Vice-Chancellor, Walter Perry. *Reader's Digest* digested him as 'a tough, practical Scot with a flair for making things hum'. Born in 1921, he was at the height of his administrative powers. He is indeed a Scot—Ayr Academy, Dundee High School, St Andrews and Edinburgh—and some of his ideas which we mere Sassenachs took to be highly original inventions turned out to be sifted from the Scottish educational system. He had been an outstanding director of medical research, and an effective Vice-Principal at Edinburgh. Walter Perry is a man of vision and drive, and it was this combination which rocketed the University off the ground and into the air. He has the capacity to be firm in practice while remaining eirenic and amiable in manner. He is informal and the last man to stand on dignity. He is a masterly administrator with an obsessive command of detail. He has learned profoundly from his own experience; he is sometimes slow to grasp the point of approaches other than his own, but he is always open to them. He trusts his own judgement, and in the early days delegated too little. A heart-attack, which fortunately proved a warning rather than a disaster, has led him to delegate more, but he still prefers to make the final judgements himself. He has been known to say, not altogether flippantly, that his concept of democracy is to give everyone a full opportunity of expressing their views, after which he can make up his mind. Fortunately his judgement is usually good. He is the University's best public relations officer; he has none of the obvious gifts of the orator, but he is an exceedingly effective advocate of the things in which he believes. All in all, it is hard to think of anyone who could have achieved more than a fraction of what he has brought to the Open University. He was deservedly knighted in 1974.

The original concept was that there should be four Directors of Studies, each associated with a different 'line'. (In the early days the University deliberately avoided familiar academic nomenclature; but it was soon felt better to insist that the University, however new in its approaches, was working to the standards of any other university, and they became Deans of Faculties.) These were substantive appointments, and it was expected that the four academic Directors with one or two others would give leadership to the whole University; they did indeed form the nucleus of an informal committee, known as the Vice-Chancellor's Committee, which met weekly over lunch and was advisory to the Vice-Chancellor. The esoteric cartoonist who invented the concept of Supa-Dean knew what he was guying: this concept fell to the ground for a number of reasons. Firstly, only half the Deans (as I shall now call them) of the initial four, or of the subsequent two, were in fact substantive: Mike Pentz (Science) and myself, and, subsequently, Walter James (Education). The others were appointed Acting Dean. Two of them subsequently resigned from the office of Acting Dean without resigning from the University staff. This of itself caused a slight problem, as the only post to which they had been appointed was Acting Dean. Their services in the University were very properly retained, but it meant that there was now no vacancy which could be advertised outside the University. So an internal appointment of an Acting Dean had to be made. It was made by the Vice-Chancellor, but only after there had been an elective procedure within the faculties concerned. An elected Dean is a very different concept from a substantive Dean. Secondly, some of the Deans reasonably felt that their primary obligation was within their own faculty. They began to concentrate almost exclusively on this, and ceased to play any great part in University committees. Thirdly, with the increase of staff the autocratic influence of *éminences grises* came under democratic fire. Deans were suspect, especially if they held substantive appointments. Yet some of us did hold substantive appointments, and had come to do a job in setting up a new university, not just within our own faculty. The result of all this has been that the present position of the Deans is somewhat ambiguous, and the part we have played in the affairs of the University has oscillated between being too large and too small: at present Deans are not members of Council, nor of the General Purposes Committee which has replaced the informal Vice-Chancellor's Committee.

Mike Pentz, the Dean of Science, is one of the most dominating personalities in the University. A university journalist sounded out the views of others about him, and discovered him to be 'engaging, overbearing, brilliant, superefficient, a robber baron, a great ideas man, a big schoolboy, and an absolute demon'. He offered a vivid personal description: 'His tremendous enthusiasm gives him the appearance, even in ordinary conversation, of a windmill going berserk under gale-force winds.' Everything about Pentz is striking, his frame, his powerful hands, his red hair, his open face, his rich voice. He is a South African, who left in 1947 because the situation was becoming intolerable for anyone who cared about people; he spent ten years in teaching and research at London University, before going to a purely research job with CERN (Conseil Européen pour la Recherche Nucléaire) at Geneva. But he hankered after teaching, and the Open University offered something new and exciting. He is still excited about it. The Science Faculty has had many difficulties, but no one doubts that Pentz has played a great part in its successes. He is a man of boundless enthusiasm and dynamic drive. He has many opponents, but no enemies; it is impossible to dislike him. He is an organizer in the modern vein; he thinks mathematically, and expresses himself through tables and diagrams. He is impatient with what he considers trivialities, like a tank crashing through minor obstacles. The integrative approach to the Science Foundation Course is his.

The other substantive Dean, Walter James, is a tall gangling bespectacled figure, with gingerish hair and reddish complexion, who came from being a Lecturer at Nottingham University. His was a particularly interesting appointment since he entered an undergraduate course at Nottingham as a mature student after a period of teaching, and was taken into their adult education department on graduation. It is characteristic of Walter James that in an article spelling out the objectives of the Open University he put first its contribution towards equality of educational opportunity at the higher education level. The second main objective he singled out was the contribution that it could make to the qualified manpower needs of society, and the third the function it should perform in responding to individual and social demands for higher education. It must be admitted that James is liable to obscure what he is really saying by polysyllabic jargon (I speak as a friend!), but when you penetrate to the meaning he is usually on the side of the angels. He is a man of principle; not for nothing is he a member of the Anglican Synod. His interventions at Senate or on other University boards are often on issues of principle; they may be abrasive, but they matter.

Walter James was a slightly later appointment. At the first stage the initially appointed Directors of Studies were invited to divide the area of work within their faculty into four, in each of which a professor might be appointed. The general plan was that each faculty should have sixteen central academics, four in each of the four disciplines, two appointed at this first stage and two later in 1969. It is vital to see that these areas of work, which later came to be called 'disciplines', are not departments. We have so far resisted a departmental structure, which would be inappropriate for relatively small numbers, and would hamper the development of an integrated approach. None the less, the selection of areas of work meant that the initial choice of staff affected curriculum development. An example from the Arts Faculty will serve. We had agreed that we would not develop language studies at the first stage. There were several reasons for this. They would not easily fit in to the concept of an integrated foundation course; we thought that their development might rest on the provision of somewhat problematical local language labs; the problems involved were very different from those involved in other areas of humanities and best seen in the context of an entirely different faculty; there was a strong sense that if languages were taught it should be for communication, and there was some debate about the validity of this within the University structure—some people argued that there were plenty of basic language courses already available through the BBC and elsewhere. My own four areas were therefore: literature, history; the whole area of thought, including philosophy and religion; and the fine arts. Plainly, the third of these was not a department of philosophy and religion. Equally plainly, the fact that we appointed a professor from among the philosophers who applied, rather than a religious studies specialist, affected the balance of later developments. Subsequently the Academic Advisory Committee advised us to separate studies in Art History and Music from one another; this had its effect on staffing policy.

The scientists chose as their four areas: biology; chemistry; earth sciences; and physics. The social scientists contrived—I never quite discovered how, but think that it was by a process of fission whereby geography split off from earth sciences (Tunstall 135 is wrong)—to persuade those in authority that five disciplines were essential: economics; geography; government; political science; and psychology. Psychology caused us some problems. The professor appointed was not a social psychologist, but a student of the behaviour of rats—important work, but not immediately illuminating the human rat-race. His work was transferred to the Faculty of Science under the biologists' wing. Social psychology continued to exist in the Social Sciences Faculty. In addition, with the development of two new faculties there were psychologists based in education and in technology. The mathematicians, by contrast, treated the whole of mathematics as fundamentally a single united area, and apart from a professor and reader in computer science and a reader in statistics, remained undifferentiated, if not integrated. When the new faculties emerged, educational studies had psychology, sociology, curriculum studies, and administration and management; the technologists made professorial appointments in design, electronics design and communication, engineering mechanics, and materials science.

Other universities had doubted whether we would have many applications, and half-expected those who applied to be the rag, tag and bobtail of the academic profession. Nothing did more to establish the credibility of the Open University in their eyes than the quantity and quality of the applicants for these first posts. Every faculty had the same experience. The number of applicants ran into hundreds, and there was no question of their quality. Professorial posts were given to acknowledged experts in their fields, men who combined brilliant research records with an enterprise about new methods in communication; junior posts often went to young men and women who had graduated with outstanding distinction and had either completed, or were close to completing, a research degree. Research degrees are not everything, but Tunstall has shown that a higher proportion of OU academics have research degrees than in most British universities (Tunstall xii).

It was soon discovered that for the preparation and *maintenance* of courses four members per discipline was too few. At the same time it became clear that we had underestimated the extent of the support services needed. The combination of limited finances and the complete necessity for expansion elsewhere has meant that no dramatic expansion of the central academic staff was possible. The original estimate, allowing for six faculties and five disciplines in social science, gives a total of central academics, including deans, of 106. Some expansion was possible, but towards the end of 1973 the total was only 221, and the distribution of a small number of additional posts sparked off a somewhat fractious debate.

One of the most interesting features of the Open University has been the interaction of academics with one another. Few of us had ever worked closely even with immediate colleagues; probably none had really collaborated with colleagues from different disciplines. It was traumatic for a philosopher to have to persuade his fellow-philosophers that he was writing good philosophy and at the same time non-philosophers that what he was writing meant anything at all, or for a musicologist to respond to a historian's question about the social and historical background to developments in music, to a literature expert's suggestions about interesting parallel developments in poetry, and to the dean's marginal scrawls insisting that Italian and German must be translated into English! Traumatic in the short term, but in the long term stimulating and rewarding. For we have all grown in the process; we have learned from one another; we do our own thing with no less dedication and sharpness, but we have learned that it has other dimensions; the experience of working as a team has been an education in itself. This sort of teamwork in university teaching is something new. It affected the appointments we made. We looked for people of independent judgement, who would have something distinctive and original to contribute, but who at the same time would be open to the ideas of others. One regrettable feature of the system is that although we have broken down the departmental barriers, the effect has been to make the interfaculty barriers more rigid. We have to concentrate so intensely on our ingroup that we have little time even for social contacts with those outside. This makes the more important those interfaculty courses which have developed, the SDT course (Science-Social Science-Technology) on *Biological Bases of Behaviour*, or the MST (Mathematics-Science-Technology) course on *Mechanics and Applied Calculus*, or the contributions of social scientists to arts courses on *War and Society* and *Man's Religious Quest*, or the development of History of Science under the umbrella of the Arts Faculty (I am perhaps the only Dean of Arts in the United Kingdom with four chemists on my staff.)

In the early days there was no Pro-Vice-Chancellor. The Vice-Chancellor's heart-attack was a warning that this state was not satisfactory. The University was left technically leaderless, with the Secretary taking the responsibility for carrying on the administrative side, the Vice-Chancellor's Committee taking immediate decisions within the University, and the Deputy-Chairman of Senate representing the academic views to Council. After his return the Vice-Chancellor appointed not one but three Pro-Vice-Chancellors from the ranks of the academic staff, to handle the areas of Academic Policy, Planning, and Staff and Student Affairs. In charge of the first area was John Sparkes, Professor of Electronics Design and Communication, a tall, sharp-featured man, who had had a varied career as a schoolteacher, in industry, as an academic, and most recently as Dean of Students in the University of Essex. (One columnist commented on how aptly his name fitted his chair, like that of Professor Rose in Biology and Professor Gass in Earth Sciences!) Sparkes made it his business to try to get order out of the chaos of academic offerings which were being proposed on all sides. He took care that the academic standards of courses proposed were properly established at the appropriate level; that there was no undue overlap between one course and another; that the range of courses offered made academic sense; and that in the eagerness of faculties to press forward with their own concerns, the importance of interfaculty courses was not forgotten. In the autumn of 1973 he became Dean of Technology, and was succeeded as Pro-Vice-Chancellor by Arnold Kettle, Professor of Literature. Arnold Kettle is perhaps the leading expert on the novel, and his appointment added distinction to the University. He is also one of the foremost Marxist scholars, and this meant that he had an important contribution to make to an integrated approach. No one doubts his standing as a literary critic; at the same time he never fails to see a work of literature in its social and historical context. This means that his sympathetic understanding ranges outside the Arts Faculty, and he has more empathy with scientists and technologists than with many arts men. In addition he is a man of genuine charm. I have known him many years, and I do not think that I have ever seen him ruffled.

The first Pro-Vice-Chancellor, Staff and Student Affairs, was Jim Barber, Reader in Political Science. Barber is a Scot, though it hits you only from an occasional intonation. He worked for some time at the University College of Rhodesia during a period of great strain, accentuated by his own field of academic expertise, and has recently published a major work on South Africa's foreign policy. He had an unenviable job as Pro-Vice-Chancellor: he found himself charged with negotiating the terms and conditions of service of all manner of different kinds of staff, some of whom had never existed before in any academic institution. It was impossible to satisfy everybody, and sometimes he played with his cards too close to his chest. But no one doubted his goodwill, and it is a noble tribute to his cheerful and eirenic personality that after all these difficult negotiations everyone likes him. He has recently been engaged on a post-experience course on the European Economic Community. He was succeeded in 1973 by Bob Ross, Senior Lecturer in Chemistry, an open, candid Australian, with a pirate moustache like Dennis Lillee's. Ross had done a notable job as chairman of the committee concerned with Examinations and Assessments, an office of considerable importance especially in the formative period, and had shown himself a man with a high concern for standards, open in arriving at policies, a firm defender of policies once agreed, and a tough negotiator. In 1974 he returned to Australia, and his place was taken by Naomi McIntosh, who thus became the first woman Pro-Vice-Chancellor.

The Pro-Vice-Chancellor, Planning, has the most thankless job of all. The office has been held with admirable equanimity by a tall mathematician, long-headed in both senses, Ralph Smith. His task is to balance conflicting claims from different areas of the University, and advise the Planning Board accordingly. Ralph Smith is an applied mathematician who applies his mathematics to planning, an expert on fluid mechanics handling a fluid situation, a meteorologist who has weathered many storms. At one point he was also Acting Dean, but he will not wish to do that again. His concern for equity and eagerness to be helpful have been insufficiently appreciated by some whose claims have had to be refused. But he enjoys the work and remains gentle, cheerful, and very firm.

Among the academic staff, but somewhat apart, are the members of the Institute of Educational Technology (IET). Similarly-named organizations may exist in other universities. I doubt if any performs quite the function, or rather functions, of this one. It forms an academic unit, parallel in many ways with the faculties; the members are actively engaged in research, and they have research students to supervise; they hope to develop undergraduate and post-experience courses. But this is not at present their most obvious impact on the general life of the University. David Hawkridge, their Director, says succinctly that their teaching concern is not what, but how. In the first place they provide advice to course-teams, individual members of staff and outside consultants on the appropriate and effective presentation of material. They are for ever telling us to spell out our aims and objectives. The challenge is an important one; how many teachers ever begin to ask such questions? We do not always meet it. We can usually define our aims; we know why we think something is worth doing. But we cannot always define our objectives; we cannot always say just what a student should be able to do after a particular piece of work which he could not do before. A mathematician may be able to say 'After working through this unit students should be able to solve simultaneous quadratic equations' (or something such), but it is harder to say what are the expected changes from a student who has just studied *Mansfield Park*. I know why I thought Socrates worthy of study, but I would not have put among objectives 'the therapeutic effects on long-term prisoners in Parkhurst gaol' attested by one tutor! None the less, the examination of objectives is important. Equally important is the advice on presentation, the use of an adaptation of 'programmed learning' (Derek Rowntree, one of the members of the Institute, has written rather a good little book in a programmed format entitled *Learn How to Study*), the insistence on clear and purposeful exercises, the initiation into the use of the computer for 'computer-marked assignments' (CMAs) which are a valuable and inexpensive way of testing factual knowledge though somewhat complex to use for sophisticated and controversial judgements, and the devising of examinations which give all candidates a fair chance to show their knowledge and critical acumen. Secondly, the IET has performed an important function in enabling material in draft form to be tested out on prospective students, and in finding the ways of recording their responses, whether in the form of general information such as the average length of time taken over a particular block of work, or particular criticisms as of the incomprehensibility of an individual paragraph. Thirdly, the research unit under Naomi McIntosh keeps us plied with statistical information, essential in an organization as large as ours, and derived from carefully devised questionnaires, on such matters as the proportion of students who watch each TV programme, whether they watch the first presentation or the repeat or both, whether they watch at home or at their study centre or elsewhere, whether they found a given unit difficult or easy, interesting or dull, how long they spent on it, and so on and so forth.

The IET has not expanded proportionately with staff in other parts of the University, still less proportionately with the proliferation of courses, and its members are not now able to keep an eye on everything that is going on. They have to concentrate primarily on new members of staff and on courses which are pioneering in new fields and new methods. There is a sense in which the more experienced academics have been trained by our IET colleagues to become our own educational technologists. The IET provides an interesting example of the interaction between staffing and academic policy. A general need was glimpsed, staff were appointed in this field, the particular staff helped to shape the University—and we have none of us been quite the same since.

There is no real academic residential community. We cannot live on top of our work because there is no housing at present on top of our work. The Vice-Chancellor for a time occupied a charming old cottage in the village of Milton Keynes, behind the local inn, *The Swan*, a mile from Walton Hall. The Dean of Science for a time was even nearer; he used to sleep in a caravan in the car park! On the whole the academic staff scattered in a circle of about twenty miles radius—which means of course that they may be as much as forty miles apart from one another. Needs and tastes in housing were surprisingly varied, and only occasionally did one hear of a househunter 'pipped on the post' by a colleague. Bedford was popular with parents of growing children because of the excellence of its schools. Surprisingly few members of the University live in Northampton, which has a pleasant repertory theatre and exceptionally fine musical traditions (we had Richter and Menuhin on separate occasions there during our first winter); on the whole they have preferred to be more accessible to London. Here the academic development of the University and the residential pattern can be seen interacting. For in the first place the University Library, excellently as it is developing, is not financed to the scale of other university libraries which serve a resident undergraduate population, and cannot hope to develop as a major research library except in limited areas. But the University is within an hour of London, Oxford and Birmingham, and not much farther from Cambridge, and those who were already living in or near these centres have often preferred to stay there. And secondly there is no regular daily teaching pattern. It is possible and desirable to coordinate faculty and course-team meetings so that, except for University committees, appearance at Walton can be limited to two or three days a week, and it may well be better, especially while Alexandra Palace is used for radio and TV recordings, to commute from London to Buckinghamshire two days a week in the opposite direction to the rush-hour traffic rather than from Bucks to London two days a week (to consult libraries and make programmes) in the midst of the rush-hour. One or two members of staff have even fled to remoter parts, Brighton, or the wilds of Norfolk, where they can write their course-units in peace, keeping a flat in London to occupy, say from Tuesday to Thursday, when they appear at the centre. The pattern of work thus affects the pattern of living, which in turn influences the pattern of work.

If the central academic staff is small in proportion to the number of students, about 1:200 or more, the administrative staff is naturally not small in proportion to the central academics. We generate many and long meetings and much paper. At its head is the Secretary, a genial, clubbable, swarthy Cypriot named Christodoulou, among other things an excellent rugby player and a cheerfully useful cricketer. His name means 'slave of Christ'; he has a Christian name, Anastasios, which is something to do with the Resurrection, but no one ever uses it, and he is Chris to his intimates and 'Mr Chris' to less intimate subordinates. Chris is chief guardian of the statutes and of the rule-book, and as such is a very Cerberus. The statutes are his Bible and the standing orders his Shorter Catechism. He is a stickler for the proprieties;

he knows the proper boundaries of the administration and keeps meticulously to them. I have seen him put up an occasional back with an occasional brusqueness, but it is impossible to be cross with Chris for long, and on social occasions he is utterly delightful. It was wholly characteristic of Chris that during a period of work on an Essex farm on his return from Africa he would be found indifferently drinking cocktails with the intelligentsia or beer with the labourers. His number two, Joe Clinch, came to us from Sussex, tall, bland, bespectacled and prematurely bald; he too has an extraordinary grasp of complex organization, and between them they make very few mistakes.

It *is* a complex organization, and involves a regular regiment of Assistant Secretaries and Administrative Assistants to service the several parts of the University, Council and Senate and the various boards and committees. The examinations section alone has a colossal task, for 42,000 students, some of whom are taking two courses, means getting on for 50,000 exam papers. Another vast principality in the kingdom of the secretariat is the data-processing division. Any institution as large as the Open University relies on a computer, whose programs have to be devised with professional expertise. The computer is responsible for student records in all their forms, for admissions procedure, for the marking of computer-marked assignments, for the evaluation of a student's results, for financial calculations, and much else. Then there is Correspondence Services, under a pawky Scot, Tom Robertson, who is responsible for the despatch of course-material to students, the communications with tutors, and much else. And of course there is the whole area of finance, under the Bursar, John Austin, which includes all the business of catering, so important alike to the contentment of the regular staff and the goodwill of visitors; we managed to secure the services of the Duke of Bedford's former chef.

New posts are continually having to be invented. In the early stages of the University we had not seen just what a complex business it would be year after year ensuring that the right material was ready for despatch at the right time. Of course, once the basic material is prepared, it is there. But mistakes may have been discovered and errata-slips may be needed. Broadcasts may have been remade and therefore may need new programme notes. Assignments must be changed each year. It is ironical now to recall that we made provision for none of this. The absence quickly made itself felt, and there were soon two administrative assistants, each servicing two faculties, and before long one for each faculty. Subsequently the post of Course Assistant was devised. These were originally intended to handle the mechanical aspects of course-presentation; they were conceived as somewhat routine administrative jobs. But they emerged at a time when young academics were chasing scanty jobs, and the quality of those appointed was academically high. Thus Course Assistants have been playing a more creative academic role than was originally envisaged; they have time off for research, and may themselves be effectively junior academics; their career-expectation still leaves open the possibility of academic appointments. Here is another example of the way in which need creates a quite new post, and the people appointed to that post shape the University in unforeseen ways.

A University which generates so much paper is markedly dependent on secretaries, and when most teaching is done by writing, and a single course-unit may go through as many as eight drafts, there certainly is a proliferation of paper. The University has been necessarily generous in the provision of secretaries. In other universities, I have known a whole department have to make do with one part-time secretary: I have known departments where no one had access to her but the professor. In the Open University provision was at the rate of one secretary to two central academics. It sounds a lot; it is in fact adequate but by no means excessive. There are obvious problems of recruitment. If you put a large organization in a tiny hamlet in the North Buckinghamshire countryside, you will not find secretaries growing on every bush. When the new city is fully developed, things will no doubt be different, but the new city is not fully developed, and when we arrived it wasn't even started. So staff had to be recruited from Bletchley and from villages round about and from as far afield as Bedford. But in 1969 there were no public transport services in the University area. Here staff recruitment had its impact on University policy in a different way. In addition to the regular minibus service to and from Bletchley station, we had to run several buses along circuitous village routes to bring staff in each morning and to take them back in the evening. A further problem arises from the competing claims of employers. The Milton Keynes Development Corporation is a rival for the girls' hands; so is the new industrial development, and they can pay higher wages than we as a government-supported institution are permitted to do. None the less the University has other things to offer. The work is interesting, and varied—in some cases very varied. The academic staff, however infuriatingly disorganized at times (and one problem about the occasional nature of our appearances at Walton is that we are for ever handing work to secretaries and demanding it back the same day), undoubtedly contains some exceedingly original and stimulating people to work with. I say 'work with', not 'work for' deliberately. Most universities do not depend on secretaries to any great extent for their teaching material. We are utterly dependent on them, so that the secretaries are in a real sense members of a team, and are treated as such; they and their husbands will be found at buffet suppers and other social gatherings with the academic and administrative staff. And though recruitment is sometimes difficult, there is no doubt of the quality and loyalty of those we have; we have had, and still have, in the Arts Faculty some of the best secretaries I have ever met.

One of the most interesting areas of staff recruitment was 'media development'. We were clear from the first that visual elements had a vital part to play in our system of education, not merely through television. Douglas Clark was appointed Director of Design (later Director of Media Development). Clark is a wiry, terrier-like Yorkshireman whose god is Sir Leonard Hutton. He came to the University with considerable experience both in industrial and commercial design and in colleges of art. He has an undoubted genius in design, and much of the favourable image which the Open University has acquired publicly is due to his unobtrusive work. He devised the University emblem, for instance, a monogram based on the letters OU, the golden O being placed with a fine sense of proportion on the blue shield formed by the U; the symbolic interpretations are almost unlimited, from an open window to a rising sun. He too designed the basic format of Open University course-material, which has won such favourable comment. Clark needed an army of artists and designers to work with him. They might be drawing graphs for the scientists and mathematicians, statistical tables for the economists, maps for the geographers or historians, isometric reconstructions for the architects, cartoons for the philosophers. They might be designing covers for units on any subject from *Patterns of Curriculum* to *Atoms and Electricity* or *Wuthering Heights* to *Functions*. He decided to go for young men and women straight from art school or college. It paid handsomely. He had fresh minds 'rarin' to go', enormous skill, vitality and enthusiasm. Nothing like this had ever been seen in the university world, and the design-team has been triumphantly successful. Clark had a larger vision, of the integration, in a single great enterprise, of the academics, the artists and the technologists. He hoped that the University would develop its own printing-works so that all the printing was done on the premises. In actual fact we do quite a lot of printing, of general University publications, and of supplementary material for students. On the larger vision more cautious counsels prevailed. But it has not been wholly lost. A publisher, Hamish MacGibbon (Tunstall 165), peering in from outside, points out that nowhere else can you stroll along the corridors, from author, past artist, sub-editor, and sometimes printer, to despatch. How many authors elsewhere can see a work at paste-up stage?

The whole area which is crudely termed 'Operations' has naturally expanded enormously during the three years of the University's teaching life. It would not be unjust to say that in early days each aspect was left to fend for itself. As the size of the operation became visible new staff were called in. It was clear that a large publishing operation would be involved, and potentially a very large one indeed. An initial appointment was made of a Director of Publishing, a woman with considerable experience in the world of publishing, Leslie Lonsdale-Cooper. One of her first tasks was to establish good relations with the book-trade; of that more later. But it soon became clear that there was a much bigger job to be done internally than anyone had fully realized. For example, copyright had to be cleared on all quotations in the course-material; all University publications had to be checked for libel. Further, academic authors varied from those whose final drafts were groomed with an eye to publication, and those who had concentrated on content rather than presentation. There was in fact a necessary editorial function, and it seemed logical to centralize this. But there were those, for instance, in the Science Faculty who insisted that their editorial work must be done from within the faculty, by someone who not merely understood science (whether or not he knew about commas) but also was closely in touch with the thinking of the course-teams. So once again there has been a creative interaction between an initial need, appointments made, and a structure which has resulted in part from the actual people appointed.

Another area of immense potential was Marketing. Again the University was slow and cautious in entering the field, and did not offer a Beechingesque salary. The problems are obvious: a government-sponsored university cannot expend large sums on what is ultimately commercial speculation, however safe the bets, and the presence of colleagues whose salaries were grossly out of touch with academic salaries would have been resented. We were fortunate to get an able and experienced man who has steadily built up this area, a persuasive and tenacious Irishman named Ernest Hunter.

As the operations area began to expand it became obvious that coordination was essential. A retired Army Officer was called in to oversee the whole area, Major-General Girling. Peter Girling occasionally wears a lost look in the mysterious world of academics, who are not as orderly and disciplined as the army to which he is used, but he has grinned and borne it, and sought for efficiency without authoritarianism. In this he has been admirably supported by the Project Control Officer, Jeremy Chapple, who has the unenviable task of watching all the schedules, and coping with recalcitrant academics—and others—who have missed their deadlines. Chapple married into the Trevelyan family and understands both the academic and the artist. Young, tall and bright-eyed, he gives something of the impression of a faithful dog—the image which Plato chose for his Guardians. He needs for his job a clear head and tact; fortunately he has both.

All this is only one part of the personnel. It was seen from the first that a national home-based university would require a regional organization, though, as with much else, the extent of that organization was not fully worked out. A central office at Walton Hall coordinates the work of the regions. The Director of Regional and Tutorial Services is a key figure. The man appointed to the post, Robert Beevers, was something of a historian and had been lecturer in history in the University of London, employed by a local education authority in the field of Adult Education, and an HMI (inspector) in adult education before his appointment to the Open University. Beevers is a tall, dark, saturnine figure, a man of considerable experience, careful to weigh all sides of a question before coming to a decision; his critics regard his solidity as an obstacle to necessary changes, his supporters claim that he contributes an essential stability and that his deliberation has prevented wrong decisions being taken hastily.

Each of the regions has its own Regional Director (RD). The people appointed were very varied and came from various backgrounds. The best-known of them in his previous incarnation was Kenneth Urwin of the London Region, a lawyer who had made a name for himself as General Secretary of the Association of University Teachers, and knew the university system inside out and back to front. They included some distinguished academics, such as Peter Salway, of the West Midlands, who was previously a Fellow of All Souls College, Oxford, and a noted Romano-British archaeologist. There were no women among the original RDs (and, incidentally, no women among the senior central academics), but Patience Burne, a former fellow of Newnham, was the original Assistant Regional Director (ARD) in Cambridge, and succeeded as RD when David Grugeon moved to help Beevers at the centre. Each RD has his ARD, and between them they are ultimately responsible for the work in their regions. This responsibility is very variously handled. Some RDs exercise a close personal oversight of all aspects of the work; others devolve responsibility on their staff and see their function in broader terms. Some are in a real sense pastoral bishops to their ministers; others see their work primarily in terms of administrative efficiency. Here again in a pioneering situation the individuals have made the job, and although there are basic operations which must be done in every region, it is good and healthy that each region shall develop its own distinctive approach and mores.

Every regional office has its own administrative and secretarial staff. The most interesting full-time regional appointments, something new in the university world, are the Senior Counsellors and Staff Tutors. I shall write later about the distinction between the Counsellor and the Tutor; here we may note that the Counsellor gives the student general advice, while the Tutor is responsible for the academic teaching within a given course. The Senior Counsellors, although there are younger men among them, have probably an average age above that of any other professional group in the University. This is right; they needed to be people of mature judgement and ripe wisdom. The Staff Tutors were selected by faculty as well as by region. There is a sense therefore in which they serve two masters, which no man can do, and they have insisted on their proper standing as academics, rather than as regional administrators. This could lead to conflict; by and large it has not done so. Staff Tutors attend course-team meetings at the centre, and some of them have contributed units to courses, or taken part in broadcasts. They have been an essential link in interpreting the courses to tutors and students, and providing 'feedback' from tutors and students to the central academics. The integrated nature of the foundation courses demanded integrated Staff Tutors. At one time it was thought that there would be one Staff Tutor in each discipline in every region. That has proved a pipe-dream, and in 1973 it was still, with a few exceptions, one per faculty per region. This meant that monitoring of specialist courses had to be carried out on a nationwide basis. Staff Tutors were chosen primarily for their care for teaching combined with the understanding that they would be concerned to see that the teaching was done rather than doing it themselves. Some of them were more academic than others; probably most of them were taken from the colleges rather than the universities. In at least two cases Staff Tutors were appointed who had recently graduated as mature students in their late thirties with first-class honours, and in one case a Ph.D. as well.

The direct contact with students is maintained by an array of part-time counsellors and tutors. These may be members of university or college staffs who might otherwise turn their hands to extra-mural lecturing or school-examining to earn their pin-money. Some of the most valuable are retired academics. (A young Staff Tutor needs considerable tact to handle some of these.) One of the best aspects of Open University openness about staff is the capacity to draw on a group of the population whose talents are greatly underused, the academic housewives. They may not have time for a full-time job; their husbands may be in a universityless area, or teaching in one of those universities which will not employ husband and wife. They have made an enormous contribution, and the Open University has made its contribution to a healthier society in finding a channel for their abilities. The part-time tutors were selected for their ability as teachers, and careful monitoring by the Staff Tutors has weeded out the less successful, for there is no shortage of applicants. The result is that the average level of teaching is very high indeed. Summer School Tutors are selected for the most part from the outstandingly good course-tutors—though others, who cannot give the time to regular work, but are happy to offer a couple of weeks in the summer, are not excluded, especially if they are from the host institutions—and are again weeded out in the light of their success in the conduct of seminars. The result is that for an intensive week in those courses with summer schools, students are exposed to teaching of a consistently high standard, such as many students at other universities may never encounter in their whole university career.

Very few tutors having started on a contract fail to complete it: only 6 per cent. At the end of the first year 32 per cent of the original tutors and counsellors were not recontracted at any level. This was partly due to a change in job-structure, partly to the ordinary process of sifting out the not quite so good from the very good, and giving new blood a chance, partly to changes in the circumstances of some of the part-time staff themselves. Between 1972 and 1973 the percentage not recontracted was 24, a substantial reduction, and not, I should have thought, surprisingly high. Over 40 per cent of tutors and counsellors served in all three years 1971–3, and over 70 per cent in both the last two.

In 1971 there were 3,564 part-time staff, in 1972 this rose to 4,351 and in 1973 to 4,729. Only about a fifth of these are women, but the fact that the average age of the women is younger than that of the men suggests that this part-time work is most welcome to intelligent women with young children. There are about twice as many tutors as counsellors, and some 10 per cent perform both roles. Rather over 20 per cent of part-time tutors and counsellors work in universities, and over 50 per cent in polytechnics and colleges of education; the universities provide more tutors, especially in science, and fewer counsellors.

Liaison with the BBC was maintained at the highest level by the presence in various University bodies of the senior people in educational broadcasting. The officer in charge of Alexandra Palace was in early days Peter Montagnon, world-famous for his production of Lord Clark's *Civilization* series. When he left to create a new series on world religions he was replaced by Bob Rowland of the BBC *Panorama* team. Leading exponents of educational broadcasting, Richmond Postgate and, later, Donald Gratton, served on Council. These names alone are enough to show how seriously the BBC took the partnership. To each of the faculties they seconded some of their ablest and most experienced staff alike in radio and television as Senior Producers, together with at least one other producer of proved expertise in each medium. But whereas the academics had been expecting to work entirely with experienced producers, and had had a fairly crude model in mind by which the academics would explain what the programme was meant to convey, and the producers would then show how to translate the programme into something technically competent, the majority of the producers were in fact recruited specially for the Open University operation—inevitably, since we could not decimate the BBC staff—and given crash-training. This may have meant, as I think the producers will accept, that some of their early programmes did not display the finesse which they acquired later. But in the end the gain was enormous. For some of those recruited were considerable scholars in their own right—one was a Fellow of All Souls—and all were dedicated to the Open University work. This meant also that they were able to become in the fullest possible way members of course-teams. They made often very forceful contributions to academic discussions; they criticized written drafts, whether of coursework or of broadcasts, with equal aplomb; they could evaluate outside broadcasters alike by the normal criteria of an entertainment medium, and by the somewhat different criteria of university teaching for mature students, who are keen to learn and too experienced to be fobbed off with the slick or second-rate. I should go so far as to say that the particular quality of those recruited by the BBC was a major factor in developing a really integrated approach to the media, so that we neither thought of the broadcast programmes as adjuncts to the written material nor of the written material as a series of footnotes to the broadcasts, but conceived all elements as integral parts of a single whole.

One point which might well be made about the Open University staff is their versatility. This is not essentially different from that of any other university, but it is a point which is sometimes forgotten in all evaluations of higher education. A number are active politically, mainly in the Liberal and Labour parties. One professor, Gerald Fowler, held a junior ministerial post in the Labour administration of the 1960s, and returned to office in 1974; he is versatile in another way, having held university posts in ancient history and political science. Some half dozen had been adopted as parliamentary candidates before the end of 1973, and others were or had been engaged in local government work. The University is not at all 'churchy'; indeed it contains a strong rationalist element; but among the staff are the chairman of the British Council of Churches Education Department, and a member of the General Synod of the Church of England. Musicians are numerous, and a fine group of wind-instrument players called the Syrinx has been formed without drawing on the professional musicians. Other instrumentalists play in local orchestras. The Purchasing Officer, Des Statham, has been national President of the Federation of Choral Societies. Andrew Rankin, the Assistant Librarian, implausibly mounted a performance of *The Marriage of Figaro* at Milton Keynes towards the end of 1973. His own performance as Figaro with his clear baritone and shrewd acting was the highlight of the evening. The Vice-Chancellor himself sings with a mellifluous baritone; he is happiest strumming at a piano and leading others. Conductors of choral groups are more numerous than groups for them to conduct. Actors are also in good supply, though nothing much has developed by way of amateur dramatics as yet. But at Brighton they still speak with awe of Brian Stone's performance as King Lear. Stone is a Reader in Literature, well-known for his translations of mediaeval poetry, a solid figure who lost a leg in Africa in the war and was awarded the Military Cross for his outstanding courage. Games are played, with enthusiasm and not without skill. An early administrator, Ted Jones, who has now moved to the Inter-University Council, represented Fiji at cricket, and there is at least one county hockey-player on the staff. Finally, one may mention that the Vice-Chancellor even in his youth floored a head-waiter by his capacity for telling one Burgundy from another.

The other, and more important, point is that there have been surprisingly few bad appointments. Of the senior academics, there have really been only one or two misfits at most, and only one or two among the senior administrative and operational staff. There has been quite extraordinary dedication to the Open University from staff of all grades from the Vice-Chancellor to the cleaners. Ennius said of the Romans of old *Moribus antiquis res stat Romana virisque*, 'The state of Rome depends on traditional character—and her men.' We might say with equal justice 'The state of the Open University depends on new approaches—and her men.'

CHAPTER FOUR

Choosing the Curriculum

We must now turn back the calendar to those early days when we had a modicum of staff and had to work out the course-content. It will probably be sensible to illustrate the process by reference to the Arts Faculty; other faculties will have had similar experiences. It will be remembered first that we were charged initially with preparing a foundation course on 'Literature and Culture'; second that I had divided the field into literature, history, philosophy and religion, and the fine arts; third that we had made some appointments, notably four professors, one of whom, Arnold Kettle, could not take up appointment till some time in 1970, and six other academics, nominally one in each 'area', but Brian Stone, a man with deep concern for students and for the process of teaching and communication, and Catherine King, who had turned from a first degree in history to work in the field of Renaissance art, seemed too good to miss, and so anticipated the second round of appointments; fourth that I was committed in the United States till June 1969 and so had for the time being to operate from a distance.

What I did was to draft an introduction to the study of man in his cultural achievement as a basis for discussion.

There was a meeting, in June 1969, of the whole University staff at Maryland, a residential conference centre not far from the University's eventual headquarters; I was unable to be present, which may have been a good thing, as my presence, before we really knew one another, might have inhibited criticism, though it has not done so since. At Maryland, apart from the general 'get-together', the Arts staff met to discuss, dissect, and eventually tear to pieces this draft. It was, they said, far too general and far too wide-ranging. This may be so, but it is of course possible to study the general through the close study of particular examples, and to focus down the wide-ranging on to narrow bands of the spectrum. What was revealed was in fact a difference of approach, perhaps of temperament. I like the broad generalization as a framework within which to fit the particular; I would rather operate within a faulty generalization (and all generalizations are faulty—including this one) than within none at all. Others prefer to start from minute particulars, without which (says Blake) Art and Science cannot exist, and only reluctantly and cautiously move to generalization. A normal university would find place for us both independently; we might meet to disagree at some staff seminar—but we might not; we would almost certainly never meet to agree. But in the Open University we had to agree before we could make any progress at all.

From July to December, with a break in August, we met several times a week for long discussions about the syllabus for the foundation course. I had to insist that we were committed to a single foundation course providing an integrated or at least interdisciplinary approach; without this commitment, which we all recognized, we might still be talking. But within it our views were various. At one end I was the one most strongly committed to integration; this was partly my classical upbringing, partly a conscious educational philosophy, and partly a temperamental liking for generalization. Close to me were Arthur Marwick, a firm believer in integration, who holds that history is all-embracing, and Arnold Kettle, who would never study literature outside its economic and historical setting. At the other end was Godfrey Vesey, who at that time was inclined to say (he has since changed) 'Philosophy is philosophy is philosophy, and you people can play at your so-called integration, but it is not philosophy', and Graham Martin, who argued for the sacrosanctity of the individual disciplines, while being interested in interdisciplinary studies at an advanced level rather than as a starting point. There were some surprises. Graham Martin himself has a first degree in biochemistry, but I cannot recall any point at which one would detect this, except perhaps in the breadth of his urbane humanity. Susan Wilson, a young philosopher of incisive mind, has qualifications in modern languages and music, but her contribution to the Arts foundation course was confined to a somewhat esoteric element of pure logic.

It would be tedious to rehearse the long debates. What emerged was inevitably a compromise, sometimes nodding in the direction of integration, sometimes a more or less successful attempt at interdisciplinary study, sometimes frankly and unabashedly multidisciplinary, with slices of the traditional disciplines succeeding one another without any attempt to relate them. This element of compromise is important. For if there were temperamental differences on the course-team, it was likely that there would be similar differences among the students, and it was important that our flaming debates should not die down into a heap of undifferentiated grey ash. We all appreciate feedback from students approving our units, and take a mild pleasure in feedback which criticizes those approaches which we ourselves reject. There is plenty of both; different approaches have inspired some students and irritated others, and it is important to have variety. One decision which we took at an early stage was that we would in general think of a single piece of work as extending over two weeks rather than one; in other words we were operating with eighteen blocks not thirty-six. Students have from time to time complained that the course is fragmented. It is far less fragmented than the average general degree or American degree in which you are for ever jumping from one thing to the next. They should be thankful that we devised the work on a fortnightly, not a weekly basis!

The pattern which eventually emerged was as under:

Introduction
1 Humanities and the Study of Civilization
2 The Yorubas of Nigeria
3 Technology, Society, Religion and the Arts: some questions
4 The Artist and Society

Disciplines and their Methods
5–8 Introduction to History
9–10 Introduction to Literature
11–12 Introduction to Art
13–14 Introduction to Music
15–16 Form and Meaning

Case-Studies
17–18 Which was Socrates?
19–20 What is a Gospel?
21–22 The Lives of the Most Eminent Painters, Sculptors and

Architects, written by Giorgio Vasari, painter and architect of Arezzo, 1568

23-24 Hamlet: a Renaissance tragedy

25-26 Descartes: the father of modern philosophy

27-28 March 11, 1829: Mendelssohn revives Bach's St Matthew Passion

Industrialization and Culture

29-36 Industrialization and Culture in Britain—an extended case-study

Logic

L1-2 Introduction to Logic

The Introduction was more or less all that was left of my original draft. We agreed that with inexperienced students we should have a leisurely run-in without written assignments, and with a very light first week's work. This was well meant, but it turned out to be totally misconceived. Students were eager to get their teeth into solid meat, and were quite prepared to skip the *hors d'oeuvres*, and they were almost anxious to be assessed. So that when for operational reasons we had to reduce the course by two weeks, it was the Introduction which was cut. We agreed that the Introduction should discuss the nature of humanities, and that it should raise questions about the interaction of history and culture, which we hoped students would carry with them through the course, and that in a course which would be, for good reasons, predominantly geared in to Western civilization, it would be valuable to remind students from the outset that there were other civilizations, which we illustrated by *The Yorubas of Nigeria*, by the accident of my having lived among them; when the cut came this had to go.

The next block was called 'Disciplines and their Methods'. This was a simple concession to the protagonists of single disciplines, but it was in fact good sense at this stage to begin to sharpen particular tools. The historians, by some hard bargaining, managed to secure four weeks at this stage. These four weeks form a highly original and controversial approach to the study of history, starting not from historical data, but from the principles of historiography. It was noteworthy, and slightly curious, that the philosophers did not ask to come in here. This section ended with another relic of my original draft, two weeks which we called *Form and Meaning*. This was intended to bring together the separated work in literature, art and music covered in the six previous weeks. We might for example ask 'Supposing you want to convey an experience concerning a tree, or concerning death, in words, paint and music, how far are the forms you use similar and how far different and in what ways are the differences dictated by the medium itself?' Or again, 'We often speak of the harmony of a painting or the colour of a piece of music. Are these just metaphors, or is there a real relationship? We apply 'ring-form' to both literature and music. Is there a real parallel? And is there any parallel in the visual arts?' In actual fact the experts in the three fields treated this as a chance to expand on what they had written earlier, and there was no meeting of minds. I 'topped and tailed' the units in an attempt to bring them together, but they were not a success.

The third block was the most misunderstood; some reviews have even treated it as if it were intended to be a Cook's tour of Western civilization. In the course of our discussions a number of areas for detailed study had been proposed. We decided in the end to keep some of them in as case-studies. They were meticulously chosen after long debate. Some of the reasons for selection were personal; it seemed foolish not to draw on my special interest in the classics or Catherine King's in the Renaissance or Brian Stone's in Shakespeare. Another argument was to include aspects of culture, particularly religion and philosophy, which had not so far been included; this was also a reason for including something from the Graeco-Roman world. All were intended to draw on what had gone before, and to bring together interests from more than one disciplinary area. To take one example, the units *Which was Socrates?*, which have been criticized by professional philosophers because they do not treat the problems which interest *them*, were in fact deliberately conceived as an exercise in source-criticism affecting the evaluation and understanding of a very remarkable man, and at the same time touching on philosophy; they could not be philosophical, because there had as yet been no introduction to philosophy. We carefully contrived that three of our case-studies fell within the Renaissance period, preceded by the two main strands of Renaissance thought in classicism and Christianity, and followed by a bridge between the beginning of the modern world and the final area of study. *Mendelssohn's Rediscovery of Bach* was in fact the most successful piece of integrated study in the course, relating as it does music to history, and the TV sequence in which Gerald Hendrie demonstrates the inappropriateness of playing Chopin on a harpsichord, and the equal inappropriateness of playing Handel on a Victorian organ, is a brilliantly concise exposition of the relationship between the two.

Fourthly, a number of lines of thought were converging on Britain in the middle of the nineteenth century. We decided to treat this more expansively, as a kind of extended case-study, under the general heading of 'Industrialization and Culture'. We brought together for this the historians, especially a brilliant young Scot, Christopher Harvie, with a passionate attachment to railways and canals; the art historians (the TV programme on 'Cast-Iron' was one of the best, showing the interaction of technology and art); the philosophers, to discuss the effect of mechanization on thought; and the literary critics, since this seemed the best part of the course to introduce a novel—they chose, slightly oddly, D. H. Lawrence's *The Rainbow* rather than Dickens's *Hard Times* or an Arnold Bennett, but in fact it provided a valuable bridge between the industrialized society of Queen Victoria's day and our own time. We had not calculated the impossibility of setting an assignment on the last two or three weeks of the course, because of the time-factor, or the way in which students would be tempted to neglect those last weeks for the sake of revision. This has led to agonizing reappraisals. Should a major item be left till the last two weeks, when it may be neglected? Or is the presence of a major item in the last two weeks the best way of ensuring that some students at least work through to the end?

In addition to all this Susan Wilson pressed the claims of logic most persuasively, as a basic discipline, a basic training of the mind. At first we built it into a two-week block to form the methodology of philosophy, but Susan Wilson claimed that you couldn't do logic like that; it had to be taken regularly in small doses over a period. So we agreed that the units in logic would run concurrently with the rest of the course. We hoped, however, that they would be somehow linked with the other units. We were perhaps picturing Susan Stebbing's *Thinking to some Purpose*, and hoping that she would take illustrations of straight and crooked thinking from the current set-books and even from our own course-material. There were good reasons against this. Logic had, so to speak, to move with its own logic, not with ours;

further, Mrs Wilson could not wait to devise her units till we had written ours. So she produced a highly original programmed, or partially programmed, course in Deductive and Inductive Logic, to run concurrently with the rest of the course in fortnightly units, but independent of it—so independent that, after the first year, we decided to put it as weekly units concomitant with the first part of the course only. This dissociation from the rest of the course militated against its success, and it has not been popular (the evidence of surveys to the contrary is unreliable, since the returns came only from those who had persevered), though those who stuck to it did well.

The course then was an unashamed compromise, but not an unsuccessful one. Its great strength lay in the principle of reinforcement. In the Introduction students may encounter a smattering of literature, say, or art criticism. They would then go into these subjects in some depth in the second section of the course. In *Form and Meaning* they would apply themselves again. In the case-studies they would have at least one further detailed study, and the same again in the final section. When we revise the course it may look tidier and more logical, but, for all our experimental gropings, I doubt whether it will be better teaching.

The syllabus once agreed, and divided into blocks, each of these blocks was entrusted to a 'working-group'. The working-group has been a useful concept in the University generally, and working-groups have been set up from time to time to study immediate problems where there is no need for a standing committee; they represented an attempt (not wholly successful!) to check proliferation of committees. Within the course-team, especially in these first courses where the course-team numbered over ten central academics, apart from others, it was invaluable; with more specialist courses and smaller numbers of academics participating, the course-team can perform the same function. In our original conception in Arts, the working-group would normally comprise: the academic (or academics) primarily responsible for the preparation of the material, another academic expert in the field, a third who, while interested in the subject, claimed no special expertise and could evaluate the material as an 'intelligent layman', an educational technologist to advise on presentation, and representatives of radio and television. With the written material we expected the writer to produce a first draft for himself, a second draft for the working-group, and a final draft agreed by the working-group for submission to the full course-team. We expected the working-groups to do their work properly, and there were usually not more than marginal comments from the course-team, such as a cross-reference to another part of the course. In the early days there were sometimes many drafts before the author and working-group were satisfied (Descartes went through eight!). Later the concept of the first draft disappeared and we were normally able to operate on a first draft to the working-group, and a second draft through the working-group to the course-team, which then with minor modifications became the handover copy.

Long before the first students had begun their studies we had to take decisions about future developments in the faculty. The Planning Committee had expected that the integrated approach would continue into second-level courses, and we followed this principle without too much argument. They had also assumed that each faculty would provide three second-level courses, so that those who were completing their degree programme without going beyond second-level could choose between dividing their second-level credits 2:2 or 3:1 between two faculties, but would have to work within more than one faculty. Our resources suggested that we could initially provide two second-level courses. There are many possible approaches to integrated or interdisciplinary study, and some of our more imaginative members wanted us to take a thematic approach. We were perhaps right to resist this. It would have been very difficult to reach agreement, and we might well have switched off as many students as we turned on. Already the foundation course had begun to focus on two periods, the Renaissance and the Industrial Revolution; these were two periods, perhaps the two periods, of major importance in the formation of our own world (I accept all that Arthur Marwick says about the dangers of periodization, and stick to my penchant for general ideas); and all of us were interested in one or the other, and some in both. It was relatively easy to find agreement on following the foundation course by A201 *Renaissance and Reformation* and A202 *The Age of Revolutions*. These were not historical studies, though they contained elements of historical study. They were attempts to look at the total culture of a period, its history, its literature, music and art, its religion, philosophy and science. The first has three main points of concentration, Florentine art, Central European religion, and

Elizabethan literature; the second asks two questions: 'How far are the French Revolution, the American Revolution and the Industrial Revolution parts of a single historical process, and how far are they disparate from one another?' and 'What is understood by Classicism and Romanticism in the arts, what is their interaction with one another, and what is common to the different arts at this period?' We agreed also that we would eventually provide a third course relating to classical civilization. By the time this was a practical possibility the concept of the half-credit had emerged, and we were able in 1974 to provide a half-credit course on *The Early Roman Empire and the Rise of Christianity*, to be complemented at some date in the future by *Greece 450–350 B.C.*

Meantime we see again the interaction between syllabus and scholar. Arthur Marwick, of all professors of history one of the broadest in outlook and most enlightened, was prepared to use two history posts to secure a historian of the Reformation, and a historian of science. To the former post we appointed Francis Clark, a former Jesuit, who had renounced his vows though not his faith, and who had a profound and balanced knowledge of Protestant theology, so much so that a Catholic reviewer took him for a Protestant; to the latter Colin Russell, author of a standard *History of Valency*, who has recently been invited to write the history of the Royal Institute of Chemistry. Russell's presence on the staff led to developments in the history of science. Other faculties were invited to cooperate, but it must be admitted that apart from the mathematicians they have done so in a somewhat perfunctory way. There are now two second-level half-credit courses in the history of science: *Science and the Rise of Technology since 1800*, and *Science and Belief from Copernicus to Darwin*. They are interfaculty courses, and large numbers of science-based students took the first, but they have been prepared almost entirely within the Arts Faculty.

Beyond the second level, students in Arts have the opportunity to specialize. We were originally eager to provide a minimum of two courses in each special area, to enable students to take two specialized courses for an honours degree. It soon became clear that many students were wanting courses in specialized areas as early as possible, and we began to think of three in each area, though this may have to be cut back. We hope, however, that some students will take third-level credits in more than one area.

At first we planned a course which would include both music and art history, but the Academic Advisory Committee wisely ruled against this, so that we have developed five areas of study, together with a proposed course on *Man's Religious Quest*, to explore student demand in that area. The initial third-level courses were in history, literature and philosophy. The history course, *War and Society*, developed Arthur Marwick's special expertise and made use of archive film. In many ways it is an interdisciplinary course, studying as it does the impact of war on literature, religion and the arts. The literature course, *The Nineteenth-Century Novel and its Aftermath*, similarly draws on Arnold Kettle's interests. The philosophy course, *Problems of Philosophy*, is a basic introduction.

The approach to the Science foundation course was entirely characteristic of Mike Pentz. Eight posts had been advertised; there were four hundred applicants. Three hundred were weeded out, and the other hundred were told that if appointed they would be members of a course-team; how would they set about designing a course? This 'sorted out the sheep from the goats'. It also gave a whole host of good ideas. Just over half the hundred were called for interview, and the eight selected were confronted with the ideas of the whole hundred, and invited to reconsider their original submission in the light of the ideas of others. This produced eight new sets of ideas. Then the entire course-team got together and spent two months in thrashing out these new ideas till they reached agreement. But the trauma of interaction was not yet over. To take one example only: the biologists and the physical scientists had their own different usages of the word 'force'. But in this course biology and the physical sciences were integral parts of a single whole. It really was impossible that students should be confronted with the same word used with different connotations in the same course. The academics had therefore to get together from the first and agree upon definitions —and this was something which in other universities they had never been forced to do. They had to keep an eye on one another too, to ensure consistency. Science made more use of the course-team where Arts broke up into working-groups. In fact the scientists described the main aims of their course—which was proudly and sufficiently designated *Science: a Foundation Course*—as 'to present and explain some of the concepts and principles of importance in modern science and to show how science, technology and society are interrelated', and claimed to show how the disciplines of physics, chemistry, biology and geology 'are related to and depend upon each other, and to show what is common, in method, technique and philosophy, and what is specific to each'.

The course starts from the 'primitive exploratory activities of simple organisms' and traces the emergence of science from its earliest beginning. This leads to the use of tools and measurement, and so (surprisingly early) to the special theory of relativity. Then in turn to force, mass and energy, and the atomic structure of matter. The course follows the line of increasing complexity through chemical bonding and molecular structure into the living organism, the cell, the multicellular organism, and the role of DNA and the general theory of evolution. This in turn leads to a study of the environment, to geology and the study of the Earth as 'a continually changing dynamic body'. Then the course returns to first principles, the nature of light and of particles, and so to quantum theory and nuclear physics, and this leads to the processes of scientific decision-making and the whole field of responsibility in science.

It is an exciting and original concept, and is one which has attracted the attention of UNESCO, which is particularly interested in integrated science-teaching. How far the course has fulfilled its promise is difficult for a non-scientist to evaluate. Some of the UNESCO experts have felt that too much of it consists in slabs of the traditional sciences laid alongside one another; in other words that it is multidisciplinary rather than interdisciplinary; and that the conception is higher than the execution. I think that the scientists responsible for the course would say that this is a superficial judgement. It may look like that, but no allowance has been made for the subtle unobvious adjustments which have arisen from the interaction of scientists in different fields, and the insistence that they all criticize one another's work.

The second-level courses in science are difficult for anyone to grasp who has not been through the travail of gestation. The basic structure is multidisciplinary rather than interdisciplinary. It consists of half-credit courses themselves compounded of two units, one worth $\frac{1}{6}$ credit and the other $\frac{1}{3}$ credit, which can be put together in a limited number of different combinations. Thus students in earth sciences can combine a $\frac{1}{3}$ credit in *Geology* with either *Geochemistry*, *Geophysics* or *Environment*. The chemists offered for $\frac{1}{3}$ credit either an organic course on *Chemistry of Carbon Compounds* (some poet devised that title!) or an inorganic course on *Structure Bonding and the Periodic Law*. Originally flexible combinations were permitted, but the decision has now been taken that the organic course can be completed only by *Biochemistry* and the inorganic by *Geochemistry*. This seemingly complex system arose out of the desire to give students as wide a choice as possible despite a slower production-rate than some other faculties. It should be added that some of the most successful second-level science courses have been developed on an inter-faculty basis, notably the exciting and popular *Biological Bases of Behaviour* (another title designed by a poet).

Three half-credit courses began in 1974, *Physiology of Cells and Organisms*, *Ecology*, and *Quantum Theory and Atomic Structure* (this last an interfaculty course with Mathematics). It will be noticed that the biologists have been able to press ahead with specialist courses more than most. But it will be noticed too that developments in science envisage much more interdisciplinary work at advanced levels than in some other faculties, and that this is an important aspect of the faculty's planning. The faculty have something of a mission. They hope to assail the snobbery of scientific specialism, which makes the training of two-thirds of Britain's science graduates irrelevant, and to restore honour to the generalist in science who will have had a first-class scientific education directed to a different end, to helping him to be a scientist in his contribution as a journalist or manager or civil servant or policeman or simply citizen.

When course labels were handed out Arts received A, Science S and Mathematics M. Social Science could not become S, and SS was clumsy, confusing and offensive. So Social Science became D, after Drake, the Dean at the time. D100 was called 'Understanding Society'. The account of the course provided by the course-team is so good that it would be impossible to better it:

> All of us understand society—to some extent. We must if we are to survive in it. But our understanding is partial, often superficial and coloured by personal experience. This course is for those who want to understand society better by approaching it systematically. We shall consider five different views of man—the economic, sociological, psychological, political and geographic—in order to highlight these various facets of his life in society.

The course is divided into three parts in which we ask three fundamental questions: why people live in societies; how people live in societies and what kind of problems they face.

In the first we ask—what does man gain from being under government? What are the economic advantages man secures through living in society? What biological, emotional and social needs does he seek to satisfy?

The second and major section of the course is focused on how men live in societies. This is not simply a descriptive account of the various social, economic and political systems which man has developed or of the environments in which he has developed them. It also attempts to analyse, explain and, within limits, predict man's behaviour, drawing when appropriate on scientific methods and skills. Each discipline thus presents a range of its insights. Many examples will be drawn from societies contrasted in complexity.

In the final section of the course we take, by way of example, one of the problems that faces the world today: the so-called 'population explosion'. This is a multi-faceted problem in the study of which all the social sciences have a contribution to make.

The summer school, through a series of field and social science laboratory experiments, provides a practical expression of the academic objectives of the course.

Understanding Society is not only a foundation for further work in the social sciences, but should also appeal strongly to those who wish to pursue other academic disciplines. For, as Barbara Wootton has remarked, it may fall to the social sciences 'to bridge the chasm between the scientific and literary worlds, which is today so widely regarded as a threat to the integrity of contemporary culture. While our subject matter links us to the humanities our methods approximate ever more closely to those of the natural sciences.'

(*Guide for Applicants for Undergraduate Courses*, 1974)

One student (Tunstall 90) described the result as 'a marvellous mix of disciplines. Having studied it, I now detest economics, know something of politics, feel involved in sociology, am entranced by geography, and can spell psychology.'

The social scientists decided to divide into their specialist disciplines at second level. They offered one full credit on *Decision-making in Britain*, and a variety of half-credits in politics, economics, geography, psychology and sociology. This provision of half-credits was popular with students; it allowed for flexibility, and the combination of any two of them was likely to lead a student into more than one area. In fact a number of students, feeling that one credit a year was too slow and two too heavy, took three half-credits together, drawing them into continuing work in three areas. A further development of importance was a joint course with Technology on *Urban Development.* Third-level courses follow along similar lines to those at second level, and once again there is cooperation with Technology in a half-credit course on *People and Organizations*, an excellent topic for such collaboration.

The mathematicians had in some ways the most difficult task of all, and it was not surprising that their course provided the highest failure-rate and the highest distinction-rate. Their task, as they well put it, was to explain not only what mathematics *does* but also what mathematics *is.* They used a picturesque illustration: if we consider individual topics of mathematics as islands, the basic concepts of mathematics are the ocean bed from which all the islands arise. In fact the course provides a *mathematical* introduction to the fundamentals of mathematics, unlike the operational approach which many of us experienced. Tom Lehrer, himself a mathematician, satirically characterized the 'New Math' by saying that it is more important to understand what you are doing than to get the right answers. I did maths up to specialist university entrance level in the 1930s, but became lost within the first unit of M100, which shows that I had never really grasped the fundamentals, but was merely a moderately competent operator. None the less, the degree of familiarity with mathematics assumed from the outset was surprisingly high. Allowance was made for the weaker brethren by Refresher Books, each covering one specific topic to the assumed level. These have no doubt been valuable, but in some ways they were a piece of irony, for the student who is already floundering is not easily able to fit in additional work of this kind. Outside the Maths Faculty it is generally held that they have assumed far too much.

Apart from the basic structure of mathematics, two topics are of particular importance in the Maths foundation course—numerical analysis and computing. Both are treated in context, not in isolation, and this makes possible work in the construction of mathematical models of situations arising in other fields and in problem-solving. This in turn links mathematics with familiar situations and displays something of its practical applications and importance. The course-team list some of the topics covered: 'Among the universal unifying concepts (the ocean bed) we include functions, equivalence relations, binary operations, morphisms, and elementary considerations of algebraic structure, such as groups, rings, fields, vector spaces, Boolean algebra. Some of the topics (the islands) which will exemplify these structures are logic, ordering, inequalities, matrices, vectors and complex numbers. The analysis and calculus areas are represented by sequences, limits, differentiation, integration, differential equations and one unit on the concepts of topology'—but they insist that these are not to be treated as isolated topics, but are parts of an integral whole. This integrated approach is the great innovation; it has been awaited for seventy years, and Technical Colleges and others have been looking to the OU for a lead.

There is no doubt that the Maths foundation course is a highly original and important piece of work. It takes account of the revolution in maths teaching across the past twenty years, and contributes to it. There is no one definitive approach to the New Mathematics; this is creative, formative and very influential.

No faculty has yet succumbed to a traditional departmental structure, but most have nodded in that direction by discriminating between disciplines. Maths refused from the first to do even that and only computing is in any real sense marked off as an area on its own. Mathematics is mathematics. The faculty is in one sense a single-discipline faculty; in another sense they might argue that within the faculty boundaries they are the most integrated of all faculties. Their second-level courses do not for the most part fall within any of the divisions of mathematics which I thought I recognized. They are full courses in *Linear Mathematics* and *Topics in Pure Mathematics*, and half-credit courses in *Analysis* and *An Algorithmic Approach to Computing* (another of these poetic titles!) The Maths Faculty has also performed an important function in relation to other faculties. Once a Faculty of Technology was established it was clear that there would be students who would take foundation courses in Science and Technology, and who would thus lack some necessary mathematics. The mathematicians adapted their foundation course to provide a second-level half-course for just these people. They also developed another course in *Mechanics and Applied Calculus* suitable for students in Science and Technology. Even more important is the half-credit on *Statistics*. It bears the letters MDET (it shares with

Science and the Rise of Technology since 1800 the credit of being a four-letter course), and in so far as the letters direct students' attention to courses rather than indicating resources spent on them, it could usefully include A and S as well. The mathematicians, as already indicated, have shown more concern than most for History of Science, and one of them, Graham Flegg, is preparing what looks to be a very interesting course on *The History of Mathematics.*

It was originally thought that technology would be subsumed under Mathematics. This slightly bizarre assumption was challenged by Lord Mountbatten when he formally opened the Walton Hall site. It had in fact become increasingly clear that we ought to have a Faculty of Technology, whatever the problems of teaching technology at a distance. The technologists were thus later in the arena than the other faculties, and their foundation course came a year later. They resented the suggestion that technology is a branch of mathematics: 'Technology is not just applied mathematics or a collection of inherited skills, though they all play a part. It is creative and imaginative, it has a methodology all its own and it is to do with people.' They called their foundation course *The Man-made World* and it is perhaps the most original of all the foundation courses. Certainly it does not look like any other basic course in technology I have ever encountered. It is concerned with human problems; it is designed to be taken by those who, without professional knowledge of technology, are concerned about the impact of technology on society. I read some of the units in early drafts—it says something about the nature of the course that they were sent to the Dean of Arts for comment, and that he could understand them—and was greatly fascinated by their treatment, say, of athletics or transport problems.

Once again the course-team succeeded in conveying vividly what they were trying to do:

> The course emphasizes three important aspects of technology.
>
> First, technologists need to use, understand, and perhaps augment the findings of research and development over a wide range of topics: physics and chemistry at one extreme, through engineering science and a study of the senses and perceptual mechanism in man, to some study of society, its cultural needs and economic and political problems at the other extreme.
>
> Second, in order to think and design creatively a technologist

should be able to break his problem down into realistic simplifications—having first taken pains to be sure that he knows the full implication of his task. This process is called modelling. Everyone faced with a problem uses models or analogies, sometimes mathematical ones, to help find solutions. But the practical aims of the technologist put constraints upon how he constructs and uses his models. Modelling can mean thinking of one's problem in a new way (the flow of traffic as if it were a fluid flow) or it can mean analysing one's problem into a range of interacting smaller problems each of which is better understood than the original one.

The third aspect emphasized in the course is that of general strategies an engineer can adopt to implement his design. The principles of feedback and control, of optimization, of linear programing and of simulation are studied; as are the techniques of systems design, quality control, instrumentation, data acquisition and computation. Wherever possible the computer terminals of the Open University's student computer service are used to illustrate these methods.

The summer school recalls and represents the wide view of technology given in the course: a view that is at once socially oriented and systematic, practical and theoretical, and dependent upon observation and modelling. They are not remedial, but provide a varied programme of experiments, workshops and visits to complement the course.

Thus, not surprisingly, the course itself reflects the nature of the broad systems engineering approach it tries to describe. The course forms a base for many later courses in science and social science as well as for those in technology.

(*Guide for Applicants for Undergraduate Courses*, 1974)

In general the faculty is concerned to foster three broadly agreed aims: to describe the nature, the achievements, the possibilities and dangers of technology in the context of people, society and the environment; to provide to students unfamiliar with science and technology some basic technological skills as well as an understanding of the technologist's attitude and approaches to problems in the 'man-made' world; to provide students with the opportunity of acquiring a qualification in some subject areas to general honours degree standard. They prefer 'extrinsic' to 'intrinsic' courses; that is to say that they like to look outward to real-world problems rather than inward to the logic of an abstract discipline; they value the case-study approach. There is a sense in which their approach is directed to responsible citizenship; they are less concerned with the solution of problems than with helping people to make informed choices in a technological age about the world they want. The faculty is divided into subject-areas. Here too the pattern diverges from the traditional academic engineering disciplines and concentrates instead on energy, materials and communication: the actual academic divisions are design; electronic design and communication; engineering mechanics; materials science; and systems.

The initial second-level half-credit courses cover a wide range of topics: *Systems Behaviour*, *Systems Management*, *Instrumentation*. In addition two courses bear the TS trade-sign, *Introduction to Materials: the Solid State* and *Electromagnetics and Electronics*, and one is labelled ST, *Solids, Liquids and Gases;* the faculty named first makes the primary contribution and bears the ultimate responsibility.

Also late in the field was Education. I don't think any of us had realized quite what the demand for OU courses would be from practising teachers. When these turned out to be over a third of the original intake, it seemed essential to provide courses in this field. They might need updating in their own subjects, but they also needed updating in education itself. A foundation course would have been completely inappropriate. Half-credits were better than full credits, both pragmatically in order to have courses swiftly available, and to allow flexibility within the field. It was difficult to find the right topics. The conventional divisions of educational studies were plainly not what was wanted, but many areas were possible in which exciting things were happening. The main divisions in the faculty represented an advance on current thinking; they included psychology, and sociology, but also curriculum studies, and administration and management. I do not think anyone from outside the faculty concerned would ever have dreamed up the actual courses proposed; they indicate a judicious and sensitive awareness of need combined with originality of approach. We can certainly here see integration at work, and the breaking up of a familiar field into less familiar components. The second-level courses are *Decision-making in British Educational Systems*, *Language and Learning*, *School and Society*, and *The Curriculum: Context, Design and Development*. The initial third-level courses were *Methods of Educational Enquiry: an Empirical Approach*, *Problems in Education: Urban Education*, and

Education, Economy and Politics. In addition there is a course of considerable importance, developed originally as a post-experience course, introduced on a suggestion from the DES (Department of Education and Science, the ministry concerned) identifying an area of need; it deals not with beginning reading or remedial treatment, well covered elsewhere, but the neglected area of the middle and higher skills in reading. Already these courses have had a considerable impact on the British educational scene. *Language and Learning*, for example, brings together psychology and sociology in an original way. Is the middle-class language (reflecting a middle-class culture) which most teachers use really appropriate or effective in a national education system? *Personality Growth and Learning* is similarly original in that, while based on educational psychology, it expands beyond the limits usually permitted to courses in this field. *School and Society* is perhaps of all these courses the one with the greatest impact. For other courses in the sociology of education have generally been structuralist in approach. This is new in its 'phenomenological-interactionist' basis. The materials of the course are being widely taken up, and there are indications that it has led to considerable revisions in colleges of education. Curriculum studies are only beginning to be recognized as a discipline, and administration and management, widely covered in America, have been neglected here apart from Sheffield, Bristol, courses at Coombe Lodge, and some direct initiative from the DES. In all these areas the OU has taken a considerable leap forward.

It is important to see that all this curriculum-planning in all faculties was carried out with little reference to students, and largely before there were any students to refer to. With the foundation and initial second-level courses this was unavoidable; even in Education there was only a general awareness that students would be arriving in this area. Need, not demand, had to be the original criterion. Later, as students became articulate, the pattern was already set. They could demand courses in modern languages or law or medicine, but unless there were substantial new funds available they were unlikely to get them in the immediate future. From the first, student-demand was larger for the arts-based subjects, national need was arguably greater in the science-based subjects. We were initially planning for something like parity, and we maintained this or something like it even when the balance of demand swung more drastically to the Arts. Even within a faculty we had taken certain commitments. If one area attracted dramatically more students than another we were still committed to both, and for all our acquired versatility could not suddenly switch off from one to another. Only when resources became scanty in 1973 and the areas with fewest students, largest drop-out, and lowest rate of production, were requesting additional resources to attain parity of course-production, was the principle of parity questioned. As I write, the debate continues.

It will be obvious that the faculty structure tended to put all the emphasis on courses within a single faculty. Within a faculty the barriers are down, and there are measures of integration that few have known before. But this very fact has tended to make barriers between faculties more rigid. We are so busy getting to know one another in the faculty that we have little chance to meet those from other faculties; even lunches are often working-lunches. We are so busy preparing courses within each faculty that we have little time to devise or participate in joint-courses. It is utterly lamentable that the social scientists should prepare a course on *Historical Data and the Social Sciences* without full participation from the Arts Faculty, but we have simply been too heavily committed in other ways. Indeed there has been little real cooperation between Arts and Social Science, and the participation of a number of social scientists in the course on *Man's Religious Quest* is a great positive gain. The science-based faculties have been altogether more cooperative. But except for the courses in the History of Science the abyss between Sir Charles Snow's two cultures has barely been bridged even in a rickety and perilous way. The philosophers are exploring the possibilities of a course on the philosophy of science, which may be one way through. All in all it is remarkable that there is as much interfaculty work as there is. But there is not enough and there is need for more. Here the initiative of John Sparkes when he was Pro-Vice-Chancellor is of major importance. He conceived the idea of the University course, to be separately financed, and thus not rivalling developments within the faculties, and to be thoughtfully devised to cover areas which individual faculties might not think of, and to encourage interfaculty activity. The project has met with general approval, but the proposals so far made seem to be bright ideas from the faculties, which can't be financed in any other way, rather than genuine University courses.

We have already noted a naive assumption that we would

write our foundation courses; in the next year we would write our second-level courses; in the following year we would write our third-level courses; and we would then be ready to remake the foundation courses. This rapidly fell apart. It depended on the assumption that eight or nine people could prepare a course in a year. This greatly underestimated the amount to be done. It took no cognizance of different rates of production in different faculties. It ignored the work involved in 'maintaining' courses already established. It probably assumed an expansion of staff greater than has in fact taken place. The cycle was early extended to four years. This was the maximum possible initial extension, since the BBC contracts to non-university contributors covered eight public transmissions (two a year for four years; because students in full-time employment would have different hours of work each broadcast is repeated), and would have to be renewed beyond that. Agreement with publishers about availability of books covered the same period. Further, some faculties felt that knowledge is always advancing, and that it would be disreputable to keep courses in being for longer than four years. As I write the whole question of remakes is under discussion. Some faculties are electing to prolong their courses in their present state for a further two years; others want an immediate remake; some are exploring the possibility of a 'rolling remake', remaking a quarter of the course each year for four years. In addition, funds have from the first been earmarked for the remake of a limited number of unsatisfactory broadcast programmes after the first year of presentation. Alterations in the written material have usually to be made by errata slips or supplementary sheets.

One other area of development is of potential importance. This is the post-experience course. It has always been the Vice-Chancellor's view that one of the greatest contributions the University can make is through the short updating refresher course for those actively engaged in a given field of work. The trouble is threefold: firstly, this is not an area subsidized by the government, so that we have to charge economic fees, which may be too high; secondly, we have no real means of ensuring that likely takers know about the courses; thirdly, it is exceedingly difficult to estimate demand. A recent example will serve. A course on the European Economic Community seemed a natural development for 1974; we hopefully prognosticated two intakes of 5,000 each; but the number for the first showing was no more than 1,498—a reasonable figure, but well below the prophecy. This has created problems for the publisher who has in good faith had printed 10,000 copies of a reader for the course. The demand for post-experience courses is at present small, and it seems best to undertake them only in cooperation with some national or international body which can virtually guarantee a reasonable enrolment. A course on *Export Marketing* proposed by the United Nations Commission for Trade and Development (UNCTAD), though it was not in fact carried through, would have been a very different proposition: so, I think, would be a course on *Counselling*, requested by a national body operating in the field, which has guaranteed the enrolment and promised back-up services.

New developments in curriculum areas are not likely in the near future. Technology was introduced because of public opinion outside, Education because of student need. The next four years, and probably the next eight, will be spent largely in consolidating the present position. There is no likelihood of substantial new funds from the government; it is always possible that one of the Foundations might support some new development. But the basic direction must be towards giving students a reasonable chance and choice within the present lines of development. The Arts Faculty is substantially ahead of most other faculties in production; yet it will be a long time before students have two full credits to complete an honours degree centring on Art History. But from January 1973 there have been potential takers for such courses.

The end of 1973 and beginning of 1974 in fact saw a major reappraisal of the University's offerings to students. Earlier in the year there had been general agreement that we were looking to a 'steady state' of 110 courses: roughly with five foundation courses, the equivalent of three second-level courses in each faculty, and two post-second-level courses in each discipline, together with some interfaculty courses. The reappraisal was connected partly with the limited resources in the operations area calling for some brake-power to be applied, partly with the fact that for a variety of reasons, some clear, some obscure, the arts-based faculties have produced material much faster than the science-based faculties. (Clear factors include the devisal of experiments and home-experiment kits, and the greater use of computer-marked assignments; but there seems an unexplained differential somewhere as compared with the musicians, who make numbers of gramophone records, and have to keep their practical musicianship up to concert pitch.) This means that the idea of two post-second-level courses in each discipline looks like Shangri-la to the scientists. The University has recently stated a minimum aim of two post-second-level courses *in each faculty* by 1976; even that will not be easily attained. The Arts Faculty had planned *three* post-second-level courses in each of history and literature for that year. For operational reasons some of these may have to be postponed. But there is a natural debate whether it is a healthy profile for a modern university to have its course-offerings so heavily overweighted on the arts side, and on the other hand whether it is just to arts students, who in any case greatly outnumber science students, to hold them back just because the production of science courses is so much slower a business.

Proposals have been made from time to time for new faculties. The principal areas have been Medicine, Law, and Languages. Medicine is almost certainly a non-starter, at least until we have some kind of joint arrangement with a medical school. We might teach pre-clinical medicine, but our successful students would have to have guaranteed access to clinical studies, which we could not possibly provide. Law is a possible starter, and the University's new Chancellor, Lord Gardiner, is one of its keenest advocates. There would almost certainly be considerable demand, not least from overseas students working in this country. Whether the country, or the world, really needs more lawyers is another matter, and it would be important to estimate need as well as demand. For the Open University is a mass-institution of higher learning on an unprecedented scale in Britain, and the mind quivers at the prospect of an output, modest by our potential standards, of 1,000 lawyers a year. Languages are a difficult area. The University is under pressure to provide courses, both from students and from outside. We have already discussed the reasons why this was not done originally. Perhaps we may see crash-courses developed on not more than a single-credit basis in communication in individual languages, though I would not rule out the possibility of a faculty of languages with a foundation course in linguistics. I have even dallied with the thought of second-level courses in the Romance languages, the Teutonic languages and the Slavonic languages; then when students came at third level to learn a particular language they would burn it up like wildfire—if any had stayed the course that long! Cultural courses could be developed between the Language and the Arts faculties.

The University has in fact followed a line of masterly and ambiguous statesmanship. There was no agreement in the University on the most desirable development; there was no possibility of attaining agreement before the bid for the triennium 1975–7 had to be in to the Department of Education and Science. We proposed 'European Studies' as a possible new area for development. It seemed topical. It neither required nor precluded a change to the faculty structure. It could embrace languages but need not do so. It could concentrate on law, and Britain's entry into the EEC raises major issues of changes in legal training. It would clearly, if I wanted to press it, cover the classics. It might merely involve a readjustment of courses already planned within the existing structures.

My own guess remains that this will be a period of consolidation. After that there will no doubt be further expansion. How long ahead that lies or what form it will take is anybody's guess.

CHAPTER FIVE

The Medium is the Message

Marshall McLuhan has made an important contribution by identifying a relation between the means of communication and that which is communicated. Our experience, even at the pioneering stage which we have reached at present, broadly supports this. Television is not, and is not appropriately used as, a substitute either for the written word or the university lecture. It has its own rationale; it presents its own material in its own way. But McLuhan's famous rejection of the printed word as outmoded in the second half of the twentieth century does not accord with our experience, and we have not been able to devise a system of learning which does not lean heavily on the written word. What we have is a multi-media system in which the written word takes its place among other approaches to learning which present different materials in a different way.

Let us begin by an obvious question and one that is often asked. How can you treat laboratory experiments in a home-based learning system? The answer to this question plainly depends on a prior question: what is the function of laboratory experiments in any system of education? Various answers might be given. They train in observation. They show how to test a hypothesis. They make possible a demonstration of experimental method by the instructor. They are an exercise in teamwork. They give the student practice in the use of tools. They make him used to laboratory work so that he can go on to advanced laboratory work. In fact none of these (and many more might be adduced), except the last, *necessitates* the use of a laboratory. A great deal of science and scientific method can be learned from a combination of garden and sky, given imaginative guidance. A great deal more can be learned from the kitchen stove: cookery is a form of chemistry. A great deal can be learned from objects to which most people have access—a bicycle, an internal combustion engine, a radio, an electric lamp. So the first aim of the scientists was to re-examine their presuppositions and ask themselves how far real science was dependent on the laboratory: I have heard one of the leading chemists say that he thinks the importance of laboratory experience is exaggerated—in chemistry of all subjects!

Secondly, the scientists have devised 'home-experiment kits'. These include a variety of equipment, some of it simple, some of it highly sophisticated, to enable students to carry out experiments at home, to bring the lab to the home, not the home-based student to the lab. The equipment is lent to students on payment of a deposit; they are also supplied with chemicals, which are expendable and non-returnable. One of the most remarkable pieces of equipment is undoubtedly the McArthur microscope, designed specially for the OU, an invention which has very properly won the Duke of Edinburgh design award. It is no larger than a large matchbox, conveniently rectangular in design, and has a magnification of 1:200. It costs no more than £5 for basic production, and represents an important breakthrough in scientific equipment. Another excellent piece of apparatus for Technology students is a 'noisemeter' or CS15C Sound Level indicator, weighing no more than 600 grams. The specially structured Foxall calorimeter is yet another triumph of special design. Other innovatory designs include the logic machine, and the CRO (Cathode Ray Oscilloscope). A simpler but delightful tool is the bobcat, a miniature pinball machine which, according to Geoffrey Holister, the first Acting Dean of Technology 'can teach the binary system to an idiot in three minutes flat'. Students in *Biological Bases of Behaviour* received in their kit among other things a lie detector, a pickled sheep's brain, and a plastic fish-tank which will help teach goldfish to tell right from left and red from blue. Other excellent devices are the 'generatorscope', a unit combining an oscilloscope, signal generator, DC supply and AC supply, enabling the student to build and test his own electronic circuit; the 'logic-kit', with which students, having identified and sorted out the logical problems involved in the construction of a traffic-controller, or something similar, can check whether they are right; various management games for the Systems course; and the prospective mini-digital computer called OPUS. Indeed, all the home-experiment kits are well and economically designed, and it is not surprising that they are in demand overseas.

Thirdly, consider the demonstration experiment. This is an unconscionable consumer of lab time, and a not highly profitable one. The student is doing nothing but watching—and even then he often cannot see properly unless the numbers are very small. Here there is an obvious substitute, so good that laboratory experience is clearly a second best. This is television. Television brings the laboratory into the home, and enables literally thousands of students to have a close-up view of what is happening. Thus television is regarded as a *sine qua non* for science courses, though this may have to be thought out afresh for advanced courses with small numbers.

Fourthly, there must be some opportunity for students to work in a proper laboratory. This lies in the summer school, and in an ideal world the scientists would like to have a summer school for all courses in science, including half-credit courses. Other faculties, usually jealous for their equitable rights, have conceded that here the science case is unexceptionable; the problem lies only in the logistical limits on University operations and the amount of time and money which it is right to require of students. It is possible that some advanced science courses in the future may be confined to those in reach of an urban area where they can have a weekly evening lab session at one of the local scientific institutions.

Turn from the laboratory to the lecture room. It is a common delusion about the Open University that we 'give lectures on TV'. We do not 'give lectures' at all. It is again important to identify the functions of the lecture in a normal university situation. It may be used to convey information, especially information which is not yet readily available in print. It offers the student a more personal learning experience than the printed word can do. It may be used for a systematic exposition at the pace of the particular group of students. It diversifies the process of learning; it's a change from books. It may be used to test out critical judgements and theories, which are not yet ready for print. It may be used for purposes of stimulus, almost of provocation. It is, in the hands of expert practitioners, an art form in itself.

The more we spell out the functions of the lecture, the more we realize that it is on the whole a very inefficient method of teaching. It is a particularly inefficient means of communicating information. It certainly diversifies the process of learning, but we have different ways of achieving this end. Unlike the seminar or the face-to-face tutorial, it isn't really personal; our system may use some personal confrontation but by definition is home-based and cannot depend on this; at the same time we can use TV, radio and even the written word in ways which are fully as personal as any lecture. We are learning also how the presentation of the written word can be prepared so as to keep pace with students: an excellent example is the type of 'programmed' presentation through question and answer, where the student who answers wrongly is directed back, the student who answers partially rightly works steadily forward, and the student who answers comprehensively may perhaps leap a page or two. There is a constraint on 'flying kites' in that in general our material is kept in print for at least four years; the general caution in this field suggests that there is a lot of irresponsibility going by the name of lecturing. It is as criminal to mislead a hundred students in a lecture room as it is to mislead a thousand by a book; but when our reputations with our academic *confrères* are at stake we are more cautious. The only essential element of the lecture which is lost is the performance of the expert practitioners. They are few and far between. Not many departments have more than one, and many have none at all. They are replaced by those with a different expertise—communication on radio and TV. They may be equally few, but the moderate performers can be improved by expert production, and the average university lecturer would not admit that he needed 'producing', though his lectures would benefit from such production. Furthermore, the use of radio and TV enables us to draw on the best communicators in their fields from all over the English-speaking world. We are not confined to those who happen to be on our own staff.

The written word remains paramount. It takes five different forms.

First there are the course-materials, booklets usually covering one or two weeks' work, though sometimes more, in a large (A4) format, popular with students but not with booksellers. They are beautifully designed, spaciously with good margins for annotation, amply illustrated, well printed. They are in fact a pleasure to handle. Some faculties use a variety of print colours to emphasize important points, or to pick out exercises, or specimen answers to them. Other faculties confine this to colour illustrations and maps. The visual element here is important. Of course, often it is merely illustrative, though even here the breaking up of masses of print may ease learning, as with the pictures of the philosophers treated in *Problems of Philosophy*. But sometimes they are intrinsic to the material, as for example in graphs, tabulations and the like in the social sciences. Those of us with a strong verbal sense are apt to forget that many people grasp a visual presentation more firmly, and even a device such as illustrating a philosophical problem by a kind of comic strip, can be of considerable help to students. Indeed it is my view that we ought in general to seek to economize on words and study more closely the possibilities of visual presentation.

But the exciting thing, in many ways the most exciting thing in the whole enterprise, has been the production of written material of a quite new kind. In the Arts Faculty we took an early decision to personalize our written material. In some faculties the work is simply ascribed to the course-team. There are two disadvantages about that. It is impersonal. And it seems to come from unchallengeable authority. An individual can always be questioned—but a course-team—? And we did not want our students to develop subservience to any authority but the truth. So we identify the authors, and we encourage them to write conversationally. We ensure that they are known to the students through radio and TV, so that students can see the face and hear the voice of the author as they read the printed page. Further, all faculties use some such device as the 'student-stopper' and the 'self-assessment test'. A student-stopper is a line across the page, which means something like 'Don't read on till you have produced to your own satisfaction an answer to this question'. The line may be ornamented; in the course on *The Early Roman Empire* we use designs from Roman mosaic pavements. A self-assessment test is a question to which an answer is provided, with which the student can compare his own response. But there is a subtler form of this, applicable where it is critical judgement not factual knowledge which is wanted. Here there is no absolute right, though there are wrong answers. So here the student-stopper performs the same function; it calls the student to a response before reading on. But when he reads on he finds not 'the right answer' but a comment on his response. We may call it 'Specimen answer'; we are more likely to entitle it 'Discussion'; and I have once ended my discussion 'I don't know what you've written, but if it's the same as what I've just suggested, I suspect that we're both thinking too narrowly, and if it's entirely different, you'd better think carefully about my suggestions and look at the evidence again.' We are trying in other words to produce a dialogue between reader and writer, a kind of tutorial in print, not a take-it-or-leave-it textbook. Of course it may become a gimmick, and of course there is nothing to stop a student from reading on without having made his response. It's his decision whether he uses the system to the best advantage. But the writing of this kind of course-material has for many of us been the most exciting part of the Open University operation.

And it has to pass scrutiny—much scrutiny. If you operate as we do in Arts, it has to pass a working-group which contains academic expertise in your own field, academic expertise in a related field, the educational technologist, and the extremely varied skills of our BBC members. It will have eventually to pass the scrutiny of the course-team. It may have to pass an external assessor: some faculties invariably use one, and much of the course-material has been subject to pilot experiments carried out with prospective students. Records are kept of the time spent over each part, and excessively long material has been pruned. Equally important has been the very frank comment of students on the quality of the material and their difficulties with it. Receipt of these comments has sometimes sparked off some amusingly explosive responses: 'What do they mean—they don't understand my teaching?' But once we realize that they do mean what they say, we have to improve that teaching. It isn't that we must lower our standards; we are a University. Obscurity is not synonymous with profundity! Russell Stannard, one of our physicists, put it well: 'I'm not going to lower the standard. I'm going to try to explain better.' Of course an academic may in the end stand by his own judgement. Sometimes in relation to a colleague he does right to say 'Well, that may be your way, but this is mine, and some students will prefer one, some the other.' But the process of criticism is one of the great strengths of our teaching system.

Occasionally we get an outside consultant to write one or more units. This has clear advantages. It enables us to associate with the written material people from other universities with outstanding records as scholars and teachers. It also means that we can treat areas outside the particular expertise of the permanent academic staff. But it raises problems. For other scholars are not used to our methods of presentation. They are used to writing textbooks, and it sometimes seems that eminence goes with a dogmatism quite alien to the approach we seek. So at the worst the material is liable to be unsuitable and unalterable, and even at something like the best it has to be reshaped at great effort by one of us; it can take longer to reshape another man's unit in this way than to write your own. All is not wholly lost. We have had some fruitful relations with consultants who are open to new tricks and enthusiastic about what we are doing—perhaps particularly when by writing several units they feel their way into the system.

In addition to the course-material there is a great variety of supplementary material sent out to students with each mailing. These may include supporting notes for the broadcast programmes. We have to be careful about these, and must ensure that they do not become a substitute for the broadcasts—still more that we are not using the broadcast medium extravagantly to present material which would be more effectively presented through the written word. But sometimes it may be useful for students to be able to refer to, say, a statistical table, or the text of a poem which is being dissected. Often it is useful to spell out the sort of questions a student may be asking himself while watching or listening, and perhaps some questions which he should ask himself after the programme in order to make sure that he has understood and assimilated the broadcast. Stop-press items, errata, corrigenda and addenda slips, explanations of material earlier in the course which has proved difficult—all these fall under supplementary material. But broadcasting notes and assignments form the bulk of it.

Thirdly, students are required to buy certain books. This has occasioned long and detailed negotiations with the book-trade, without whose cooperation the success of the University would be impossible. If we are to prescribe a book for a course lasting four years, we require guarantees that the book will be available throughout the period of its prescription, and that there will be no unreasonable rise of price during that period; we would also like to see it available as cheaply as possible for our students. After an initial period of slightly suspicious manoeuvring the University and the two associations principally concerned, the Publishers and the Booksellers, have come to a mutually advantageous agreement and considerable mutual confidence. Only with some American publishers, who operate somewhat differently, has there been any serious problem about availability, and only one publisher has raised his prices contrary to his agreement with the University, above levels explicable through rising costs. All we can do in such cases is to advise course-teams that that particular publisher has broken his agreement, and, other things being equal, his books should not be prescribed—but other things are not always equal. Similarly, the University has once been at serious fault in an over-optimistic guess at enrolment; the publisher was warned immediately the signs were apparent, and it proved possible to find a way through what might have been a very difficult situation. With an enrolment of about 5,000 in some foundation courses, there is a guaranteed sale of 20,000 over four years, which makes possible a lowered price, or perhaps the conversion of hardback to paperback. But the lowered price in turn helps sales outside the University. So there are advantages alike to our students, the book-trade, and the general public. Any course with 1,000 students is likely to generate sales of at least 5,000. Even a low enrolment of 250 offers guaranteed sales of 1,000, which is certainly a basis for keeping a book in print. With the helpful cooperation of publishers we were able to keep necessary student expenditure on set books down to £10 for each foundation course, and £15 for each subsequent course, though with rising costs we have had to allow some courses to move towards £20; this last is only done after scrutiny of each individual item. Naturally we would like students to be confronted with a variety of views, and enriched by diverse reading. But we are also conscious that our notional 'basic' student does not read fast and has not much spare cash. If he reads twenty pages an hour—quite fast for academic material—and spends six hours a week on reading, he may reasonably cover some 4,000 pages in a year. Probably half of this reasonable allocation will be taken up by course-material and supplementary material. We tend, especially in the arts-based subjects, horribly to overweight our students' reasonable reading capacity. Further, our present prescription levels mean that a student may have to pay £80 for books for his basic degree, and £110 for his honours degree. It is doubtful whether we ought to demand more. For these are books which a student must buy and possess.

And be able to get. The other side of our negotiations with the book-trade has been with the Booksellers Association. It was tempting to 'go it alone' and establish our own mail-order system for students; one colleague even suggested an Open University

Book Club with reduced rates. There were cardinal reasons against this. It would have been an immense operation which we could not have mounted in the time. It would have required vast warehousing, clerks, packages, accountancy. It would have involved capital expenditure we could not reasonably undertake with public money. It might, with rising costs of postage, have proved more expensive for students. Further, we wanted to be on good terms with the book-trade, and we wanted our students to be the sort of people who would go into bookshops. So we worked closely with the Booksellers Association. They invited their members to opt to become Open University Stockists. These guaranteed to keep foundation-course books in stock, and a student would know that he could find what he wanted. Later, as courses proliferated, some of them with small numbers, there came the concept of the regional stockist, who would keep all OU titles in stock, and supply them promptly either direct to students or to other booksellers in the vicinity. This has worked excellently: in 1973-4 there were 280 stockists and 36 regional stockists.

Among these prescribed books falls the fourth category. These are books originating in the Open University, and tendered for by publishers competitively. For the most part they are readers, collections of primary sources or secondary criticism put together with appropriate comments by members of the course-team. An outstandingly successful example is *Understanding the Earth*, a reader in earth sciences for S100, and an altogether brilliant piece of editorial work. These readers have to be a substitute for access to journals in university libraries; the best students lose the chance of comparative browsing, but far more students read the articles. Such readers are not as easy to compile as might at first appear. They have to be completed twelve months before the course begins: their basic design must be known for tendering purposes some little time before that. But much of the course is not written at that point, and it may not be clear what is needed. They are nearly always compiled against the clock. They nearly always tend to be too long; it is reminiscent of the preacher who said that he would have preached a shorter sermon had he had longer to prepare. Further, for them to interest publishers, they must normally be good books in their own right, of interest to other than OU students. Sometimes the requirements of teaching and the requirement of general interest pull in different directions. In *War and the Creative Arts*, for example, two of my colleagues came to me after my original closing date, but before the handover to the publishers, with inordinately long passages which they were using for teaching, and which altered the balance of the thing. Of course teaching had to come first, but it required much delicate trimming to restore an adequate balance, and a review which commented adversely on the fact that some of these passages (forced on me) did not fit the anthology really hurt. The size of the operation has meant that prices have been very reasonable throughout and for the foundation course extremely low. My *Socrates: A Source-Book* was reasonably criticized by reviewers because we used cheap paper, double columns, and (for reasons of economy and speed) out-of-copyright translations. But, for all its faults, we did succeed in offering the reader 335 double-column pages for 41p—and as that included the first translation of Libanius's *Defence of Socrates*, which alone would normally have cost £2 or so, it was something of a bargain. The process of evaluating tenders is an interesting one. Naturally we veer towards the lowest, if we are persuaded that it is realistic. But we need to be sure that the publisher is adequately equipped in the areas appropriate to the particular work; a book with many quotations requires a good copyrights department; art illustrations and scientific or mathematical symbols demand their own expertise. We have discovered by experience that it is unwise to entrust more than two books to any one publisher; we are anxious in any case that the University is not monopolized by a single firm. We look too at whether a publisher will have good general sales in that area, for we are primarily but not solely concerned with our own students. We use the Open University Press only when the book is composed of material already published by the Open University and not likely to appeal to the general public; if the Press grows and casts its net more widely, its tenders will be discussed on the same basis as any other.

The readers have occasioned a mild conflict between some members of the academic staff and the University. The Council was from the first anxious to avoid the charge that members of the staff were feathering their own nests by receiving royalties from books which they themselves prescribed to a very large captive audience. The University receives a royalty on the readers, which may be as much as 10 per cent. The Council ruled that editors of these readers should not receive any of the royalties, but should receive an appropriate honorarium. This was defended on three further grounds: the impossibility of a complete separation of these readers from the preparation of course-materials as a routine duty; the fact that readers for small courses should be rewarded equally with readers for large courses; the swingeing tax on payments to individuals which made it more appropriate to use the royalties for the general benefit of course-teams. Not all editors see it this way, especially when their work has wide sales outside the University.

The fifth aspect of the printed word is background reading. Each unit, and each course (as a collection of units), may have a list of recommended reading or background reading. These are likely to contain some books cheaply available in paperback, which many students will wish to possess; they will also contain books, some perhaps out of print, which students can consult in libraries. These are not required reading, but valuable enrichment. These lists are available to booksellers, and an enterprising bookseller can use them to good effect when students come in for their set books. They are also available to libraries. In general, however, students have made less use of libraries than librarians hoped or feared; for the most part they scarcely have the time. But these lists may be permanent possessions, and a great help in following up in later years topics which have proved of interest.

The second medium used by the University is broadcasting. It is exceedingly difficult to generalize about the use of broadcasting; it has been used very variously by different faculties, and even within a single faculty. But one or two general points may perhaps be made. First, for the student who is not used to academic work television is a vital bridge from the familiar to the unfamiliar; the *average* time each week spent by the adult Briton in watching TV is 16½ hours. Secondly, television and radio, as mentioned just now, perform a 'Meet the Faculty' function. I remember right at the outset saying to my BBC colleagues: 'Look, if we're hopeless performers on radio and TV, you must just tell us so; and if you won't, tell me, and I will. But however bad we are, students must see what we look like and hear our voices, otherwise the whole thing will become impossibly impersonal.' Thirdly, both radio and television can be used to introduce students to leading authorities in any subject from outside our own staff. This has been a particular feature of *Problems of Philosophy*, in which most of Britain's leading philosophers participate in one way or another.

The Education Faculty have a characteristically well-thought-out attitude to the use of broadcasting and have identified three different ways in which broadcasting may profitably be used. Firstly, in most teaching the teacher comes between the student and the subject. Broadcasting, and particularly television, enables the teacher to stand aside from the visible role of middleman. He has of course been there all along, planning the programme. But on the face of it the student appears to be confronted directly with a situation, especially if the teacher can resist the temptation to superimpose a commentary. (The social scientists exercised this self-denying ordinance in their programme on Chicago.) Secondly, most teachers, once launched, are frighteningly isolated. Both television, and, where the visual element is unimportant, radio can expose the student to a variety of experience and a variety of method. Thirdly, it proved possible through radio and TV to introduce students to a variety of people of valuable insight and experience—not only academic but also, for example, those involved in the processes of decision-making such as Margaret Thatcher and Shirley Williams.

The mathematicians have made particularly brilliant use of television in the foundation course. In the first place they have used television to link abstract mathematical problems with real-life situations. Thus one programme begins with a visit to an air-field, and a problem (I think) of the flow of petrol into the engine of a jet-aircraft; this leads to the study of the solution of a particular type of equation. Another programme starts from an oil survey and leads into the geometry of surfaces. The other very striking aspect of the maths programmes is the use of animated graphics: even such a simple device as the growth of a line of light connecting the points of a graph, is an impressive reinforcement. Perhaps the purest of mathematicians would say that this is a concession to weakness, as Plato thought the use of visible figures inferior to the direct grasp of truth. But the mathematics course must cater for the less pure as well, and for the layman these animated graphics are a superb teaching aid. There were twenty-nine computer animations in M100. The mathematicians have found it much less easy to find a real use for radio; they have used it for mathematical history, and outside contributors have made notable contributions—but students do not listen to non-examinable talk.

The technologists are not unlike the mathematicians in one

respect. Their primary use of television is to relate their technology to real-life situations. Radio is of particular value for the presentation and promotion of discussion. Similarly the social scientists see broadcasting principally as a means for the presentation of case-studies, an important aspect of social science, and one entirely apposite to the medium. Here sociology comes off best, though geography offers enormous scope, sometimes hampered by the problem of recording voices in exposed places. Scientists, as we have noted, see television as an essential component of their courses, because it is an unusually effective means of presenting demonstration experiments.

In the Arts Faculty we have not found any simple formula, and this is perhaps right. Plainly it is appropriate to use radio where something must be heard, television where something must be seen. That might seem platitudinous but the obvious is sometimes forgotten. Music must be heard: a radio programme is valuable for the dissection and analysis of a piece of music. But sight may here reinforce sound, and the brilliant piece by John Dankworth introducing the instruments of the orchestra is television at its best. Something similar was done with the unfamiliar instruments of Renaissance music, and, at a more advanced stage, with the baroque organ. Art and drama might seem obvious candidates for television, but not in an obvious way. For not all students have colour television, and a picture cannot be left indefinitely on the screen; a colour reproduction may be better for students to study. Television is at its most useful in ranging round architecture, or in studying different uses of a medium, as in the foundation-course programme on cast-iron already mentioned. So with drama. It must be heard and seen. But TV programmes last twenty minutes only, and it would take ten programmes or more to present one Shakespeare play. So it has to be used more subtly, on an isolated theme, like 'The Fool in *Lear*'. Dramatizations of novels may be counterproductive and anti-educational; they may supply an image which should arise from the student's reading, and distract from the author's gift of creating his effects through words. Arnold Kettle has, however, two masterful programmes, which ought to be compulsory viewing for TV addicts, taking excerpts from TV serials and discussing their difference from the novelist's intention. Television may usefully recreate a background to an author's life, Lawrence's upbringing among the mines, the moors of Haworth, the Kent marshes which form the background to the early chapters of *Great Expectations.* More subtle and brilliant is the programme on 'improvement' as a focal theme in *Mansfield Park*, showing visually what was happening to large private gardens, and suggesting parallels with the moral theme. So too with Zola's *Germinal.* John Berger went into a Midlands mining community from outside, much as Zola did in his own day, and commented on how far he could enter into the life and how far he felt excluded; it will not have been so different for Zola. This last was a programme of rare imagination and insight. *War and Society* used television quite differently. Here the moving visual image was treated as a primary source, and the television programmes consisted of the presentation and criticism of archive film. This again is a piece of pioneering teaching.

Television then has had very varied uses. Radio has been a little more straightforward. One of our early programmes was a direct talk, almost a mini-lecture, by the Provost of King's College, Cambridge, brilliant in its way, difficult, stimulating, but perhaps unrepeatable. We have tried unscripted discussions between visiting scholars. At its best this is an important teaching aid, presenting students with a diversity of views and disagreement between authorities, but such discussions are liable to run away into arid sand. Question-and-answer sessions, prepared but unscripted, are better; the questions control the discussion, and in one instance a very long session allowed the irrelevant and impertinent to be omitted by subsequent editing. Dramatizations have a part to play. A programme called 'The Princess and the Philosopher' used Princess Elizabeth as a highly articulate foil to bring out and challenge some of the views of Descartes, and in philosophy (which Plato called 'dialectic') this approach offers considerable possibilities. Probably all in all, however, the most effective use of radio is the straightforward talk, with verbal illustrations read in by one or more actors. I have used this myself for subjects as diverse as Socrates, Francis Bacon, the Cambridge Platonists, Stoicism in Seneca's tragedies, and Martial the epigrammatist. It is interesting how excited the BBC actors are by the chance of participating in something a little out of the ordinary line of business.

One problem about broadcasting has been the shortage of suitable times for presentation. Entertainment takes over from 7.30 p.m. on weeknights, and from Saturday and Sunday afternoons. It is of course possible to find air space on a weekday by pushing back into the afternoon, but our students are for the most part in full-time employment, and listening and viewing figures plummet the further we recede from 6 p.m., let alone 5 p.m. It is also possible to use the very early morning, and certainly some students find 7-8 a.m. very attractive; I cannot think that many are similarly enamoured of the period 6-7 a.m. We have thirty hours guaranteed for both radio and TV at regular times each week, subject only to incisions from Wimbledon, Test Matches, Open Golf, 'party conferences or other sporting events of national importance' as the agreement delightfully puts it. A displacement for a promenade concert which started half an hour early occasioned a confrontation, especially as the concert was available on another programme. There has been no further crisis. The University's insistence that all programmes should be repeated has complicated the scheduling. Without this it is impossible to guarantee that students taking more than one course will not have a clash between a radio programme for one and a TV programme for another. The doubling was originally to give students with awkward hours of work a second chance. In fact it turned out that 80 per cent of our students listened to the first presentation whether it was on a weekday evening, or at the weekend. But a significant number liked to hear the programme twice—and it should be remembered that even if 10 per cent cannot hear one of the presentations, this, although a small proportion, is 1,500–2,000 out of each year's intake.

Plainly, our problems of presentation would be greatly eased if a fourth TV channel became available for educational purposes. The senate did in fact pass a motion asking for a fourth channel to be directed to community and educational uses. We certainly do not want—or rather could not afford to want—a channel to ourselves. But we could do with a slice of time after 7.30 p.m.

Other developments in audio-visual presentation are forecast. One which occupied our thinking in early days, and may do so again, is the development of cheap videotape playback facilities. At one time it looked as if we would have to back one or other of the rival systems before they were proved. Fortunately we temporized. I do not think that this is a real option. It does not touch production costs, which form between 15 and 20 per cent of the broadcasting bill, or overheads, which swallow up 75–80 per cent. Transmission costs are only 5 per cent. But even if the mystic 'black box' comes down dramatically in price, videotape will still cost money—and every student will need a simultaneous copy. Nor will the possibility of cheap off-air recording-machines help much, for the programmes have still to be presented on open circuit. These do no more than allow programmes to be broadcast at less favourable times and watched at a student's own convenience; this is an advance, but one which involves no saving in money. I think it more likely that open circuit television will come to be supplemented by rather different audio-visual devices, such as the filmstrip linked to an audio-tape and fed through a viewer at a controlled speed. We have not even experimented enough with radiovision, the linking of a radio programme to visual material sent separately to the student.

The study centres are an important ingredient of the system. There are just under 300 of them, and it seems that about half our students use them at least once a fortnight. They offer four main facilities. First is the opportunity to get together with other students. The study centre thus can provide something of a substitute for college life, and it is good that some study centres have developed a life of their own. Even where there is not a study centre, self-help groups have sometimes developed with students visiting one another's homes. The OU system must be valid for the isolated student, the famous notional shepherd on the island of Mull (whose name, I am told, is almost bound to be MacLeod). But he must be very isolated indeed if there is not a single other student in reach. This learning from one another through mutual discussion is an important contribution to the pattern of education, which one would like to see more widely practised. I recall the words of young Peter Lapwood when he came out of China into an English school, and was asked the difference between the two systems of education; he said: 'In China they taught us to cooperate; here you teach us to compete. There if anyone was in difficulties we'd all join together to help him; here you call that cheating.' The OU self-help group is at least a contribution towards cooperative education. Second is the provision of facilities for seeing and hearing programmes together with not very satisfactory video-cassettes and rather better audio-tapes of earlier programmes. These facilities were in some demand at the start, and we had rather conceived students as receiving programmes together and then discussing them; indeed in the first year Arts academics made a point of being in a study centre when their programme was on the air. In fact about five-sixths of our students prefer to watch programmes at home. And this is right. The OU system is designed for home-based learning. The study centre is a valuable adjunct. But the study centre tail must not wag the OU dog. Besides these, the study centre offers the opportunity for regular consultation with a counsellor and occasional encounter with a tutor.

The life of the study centre depends in no small measure upon the work of tutors and counsellors. The primary function of tuition is relatively clear. It is an academic function related to a particular course. It may include correspondence tuition, assessment, face-to-face tutorials and communication and interaction with students in different ways. Originally in the Arts Faculty we sought for generalist tutors to cover the correspondence tuition, and for the occasional encounters with students at study centres we thought there ought to be a succession of specialists. This didn't work, partly because the visiting academic who only met the students once in a year didn't feel sufficiently identified with them, or with the University, partly because students had no other chance of meeting their correspondence tutors. So the work of correspondence tuition and face-to-face tutorials has been increasingly vested in the same person. Counselling is a much less easily definable function. Some people have analysed it into academic counselling (advising students about study methods in general, encouraging self-help groups, and encroaching in a strictly limited way upon the tutorial role), pastoral counselling (relating to personal student problems), and administrative counselling (interpreting the system to students), but others see this analysis as unrealistic and misleading. There is no doubt that the success of the system depends upon 'a clear understanding by both tutor and counsellor of their distinct functions'. There is also no doubt that the functions are not always distinct, and the offices of tutor and counsellor have tended to come together, despite efforts to keep them apart.

One of the part-time counsellors has given a vivid characterization of her work: 'My job as counsellor is to make coffee, listen to grievances, encourage the despairing, help those who have struck real trouble in their work, take part in discussions on Zola or Calvin, Blake or Machiavelli. Above all, I have to try to draw my amazingly disparate students into a community of learning.'

But the major opportunity for students to meet with one another, and with expert tutors, is the summer school. All the

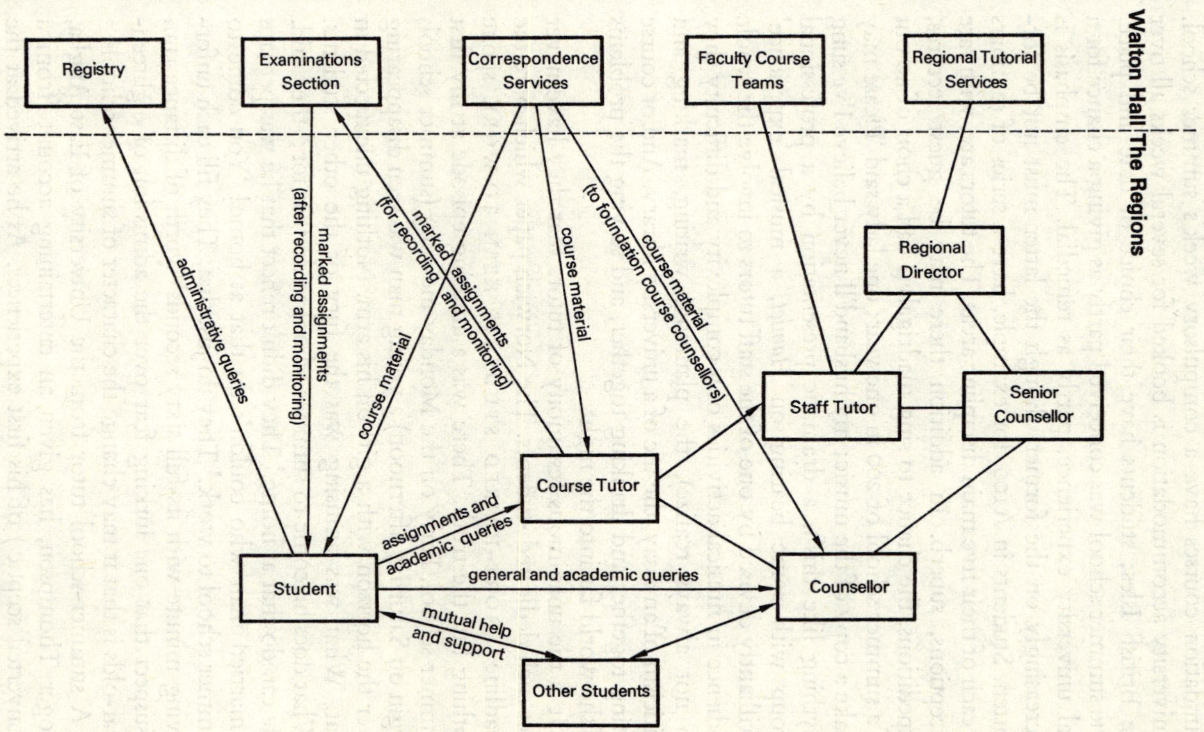

FIG. 3 Communications within the University (from *B.A. Degree Handbook*, 1974, p. 59)

foundation courses have a compulsory week's summer school. University accommodation is booked for several weeks all over the British Isles; students have their choice of date and place. The summer school was conceived partly as giving a chance for a real university experience, partly as remedial. The emphasis is increasingly on the former, though the latter must not be forgotten. Students in A100, for example, have a series of seminars in each of their five main discipline areas. The tutors are, with rare exceptions, superb. In addition there may be guest lectures, expeditions, the chance to sing madrigals (I had a choir of 40 out of a summer school of 200 in one year; one lady said 'Please may I take a copy of the music; my husband'll never believe I've sung anything like this'), a dramatic presentation by a professional group with some bearing on *Hamlet*, a musical 'experience' (brilliantly devised by one of the staff tutors to involve the whole audience in musical activities of a complexity and difficulty they do not always realize), the planning, writing, marking and criticism of an essay, the use of a university library. And of course eating together and drinking together, and solving the problems of the world far into the night.

It is the unanimous testimony of tutors that they have never met such dedicated students. The Norwich paper which bore the headline SHORT-HAIRED STUDENTS KEEN TO WORK spoke nothing but the truth. There was a amusing episode at my first summer school. Early on the Monday morning (summer schools begin on Saturday afternoon) a young man was seen disappearing over the horizon with a girl on his arm. Nothing unexpected in that. What was amusing was the fury of the other students. 'What does he come to summer school to do that for?' they said. 'He can do that at home.' They didn't reflect that he was perhaps a married man who couldn't do that at home! 'You come to summer school to work.' They do just that. They fill each unforgiving minute with its full sixty seconds' worth of distance run. I suspect that one lurking fear over the admission of eighteen-year-olds is that it may change the character of summer schools.

A summer-school tutor from the University of East Anglia, Roger Thompson, has given an entertaining account (from a 'converted sceptic') of his first experiences. As he arrived at the familiar campus he found Open University notices everywhere. The emergence of two Martians from a tree-stump seemed too much: they turned out to be only wasp-exterminators. He describes the mix of students: 'company directors and city councillors, pilots and priests, housewives and hairdressers, pregnant mothers and men from the Pru, social workers and salesmen, journalists and Justices of the Peace, doctors and dog-breeders, artists and antique dealers, one lady who would rather not say, and one university lecturer. A man horribly crippled zoomed startlingly round the walkways in his three-wheeler; a blind lady's guide dog hardly ever snored in seminars.' Thompson found the first encounter with a seminar group a little daunting, but by the end of one and a half hours they were hard at the issue of individual initiative versus vast impersonal historical forces. Intelligence varied, though there were not many fools, and not a few first-class brains. What did not vary was the friendliness, tolerance, eagerness to learn, determination to participate positively in all the activities of the week, responsiveness, sense of fun, and stamina. He gives a wonderful picture of his most difficult group, with an Anglican school chaplain, 'who spoke as though he were addressing an open-air congregation of thousands in a high and contrary wind'; a retired international civil servant, 'currently engaged on historical research the like of which mere mortals such as we would never appreciate', who wore his grey hair in a pony tail; a 'neurotically uptight spinster who refused to reveal her forename, hometown or intended specialization'; an unemployed printer who cast himself as 'cheekie chappie'; and a primary school headmaster 'who opened a huge notebook and produced four immaculately sharpened pencils'. Yet, even after this unpromising beginning, by the end of the week 'the chaplain boomed less, the pony tail seemed to have something to learn, the uptight, if not exactly downloose, no longer flared her nostrils when the sobered printer spoke, and the notebook had disappeared.'

It was evident to some from the first that it would not be physically possible for the University to mount a summer school for every course. It was doubtful whether it was fair to try to do so. Not everyone could easily take a week from his holiday for every course. If he was taking two credits in a year he might be absorbed for two weeks out of a three weeks' entitlement. Further, it would cost him £70 or more even without travel, and though the local education authorities might pay these costs they do not always do so. For scientists the summer school provided the only real chance for laboratory work. Plainly they have every right to priority here, though it was a mistake to seek, as they did at one time, a week's summer school for each half-credit course. The Arts Faculty did not offer summer schools for second-level courses, organizing a series of day-schools instead, but made them a compulsory part of the first specialist courses at third level. Different faculties have evolved different patterns, but the optimum number of summer schools seems to be about six or seven in a faculty.

The basic help to students is given by the correspondence tutor, and correspondence tuition is a major part of the system. In specialist courses this creates no problem. But in courses which even nod in the direction of integration there is a dilemma. On the one hand students will benefit by having a single tutor to watch and guide their progress. But no single tutor is likely to have mastery of the whole of one of our foundation courses, let alone our second-level arts courses. Different faculties solved this in different ways. In S100 (100 designates a foundation course, 2-- a second-level course, and so on) the course really falls into four blocks, physics, chemistry, biology and earth science, and a separate tutor can cover each block; in any case, the scientists made far more use of computer-marked assignments. In A100 we took a different view. We felt that at this level continuity of guidance was not merely desirable but essential. We thought that we could not in conscience ask students to master a course which no one could teach. We also realized that if integration and an interdisciplinary (as opposed to a multidisciplinary) approach meant anything at all, we could not make our assignments narrowly specialist. So, despite raised eyebrows in some places, we have course-tutors. We give them 'tutor notes' to guide them outside their areas of greater expertise. These shackle the weaker tutor, but, provided they are treated as guidelines not bonds, are a valuable though time-consuming part of the system. Altogether it has worked well. There *are* disadvantages, but they are greatly outweighed by the advantages. At the second level, with its sterner intellectual demands, we have compromised. We have asked tutors to cover as much of the course as possible. But we have, we think rightly, insisted that such areas as Renaissance music, or Kant, must be taught by someone with specialist knowledge.

The work of tutors is monitored by staff tutors, and there is continually consultation between different members of the full-time staff: a particularly important consultation was held at Maryland (the conference centre mentioned earlier) in 1973. Tutors make marginal running comments on the work they correct, and a general comment on a form (known as CT3). Both require considerable skill. For example, in a mathematics exercise an underlining shows that something is wrong without showing what is wrong, but a concise verbal explanation is not always easy. The general comment 'Please try to improve your style and structure' is not very helpful: the student needs to know exactly where his style and structure are defective. An A-grade student may require astringent comment matched to his A-grade; those floundering need gentleness without flattery. (I had a letter from a non-English student: 'My tutor says I am brilliant; why does he give me a D?') A comment from a maths tutor which was agreed to be pitched right for the first assignment of M100 ran 'A very good answer to Q8. Well done! Your attempt at Q1 was also good and you almost achieved the correct solution. It was a pity you omitted the condition for composition of 2 functions (please see my comments on the script). I hope your mark on Q5 will not depress you. Unit 3 causes difficulty with all students, but the ideas will gradually become clearer as you progress through the course. This was quite a good first assignment, and I look forward to seeing more of your work.' Here the correlation with marginal comment, and the personal note, are particularly commendable. In general the monitoring procedure has been invaluable alike in rising standards, in helping to achieve consistency, and in weeding out the sheep to be offered reappointment from the goats.

Anything like a final degree examination was out of the question, even had it been desirable; the possible combinations of courses were too complex. Each course had to be separately accredited. The University early decided to climb on the bandwagon of continuous assessment, which was the fashionable panacea for examination fever. There are three problems about continuous assessment. Firstly, so far from taking the sting out of examinations, it is liable to turn life into a perpetual examination. We eased this by an administrative innovation. Students are assessed on the best two-thirds of their work only. This makes it possible for them to relax, to chance their arm on an experimental approach rather than playing safe, to avoid penalty during a period of illness, and to carry a blind area in a multidisciplinary course. It also means that in a course involving ten essays (about the norm for a full-credit course) once they have seven good marks tucked under their belts they are liable to neglect the last three assignments. In general, however, this is an enlightened provision. Secondly, the fact that all work is assessed pulls against educational values. A tutor writes in and says, 'I have a student who is floundering, but not hopeless. He can't cope with the official essays. Can I set him instead something suited to his present needs?' We have to say 'No' and it is a shame that we must do so. Similarly, in a normal situation if a student is below standard the moment I see a gleam of light I give him a pass mark. He hasn't earned it, but the chances are that, with the encouragement, in another three or four weeks he will. But with continuous assessment we have to instruct our tutors not to do this. Thirdly, with continuous assessment and teaching at a distance it is impossible to be sure what help a student may have received from outside. Student self-help groups working out their assignments together are educationally an important development. But we still have to accredit individual students.

Assignments are of two kinds, Computer-Marked Assignments (CMAs) and Tutor-Marked Assignments (TMAs). The former are widely used in the science-based subjects. They are excellent for mathematics, excellent also for the testing of factual knowledge. When numbers are large they are cheap to administer, and the computer which marks them is subject to none of the subjective variables which notoriously affect the human marking of essays. They can be used to test critical judgements, but such CMAs are a major task to construct, and it is very difficult to avoid imposing the judgements of the constructor. In the Arts Faculty we have found a valuable use for the CMA in enforcing re-reading or revision to find the answers to straightforward questions. But as any conscientious student ought to achieve 100 per cent on this exercise, it is of little value for assessment purposes. Even a straightforward CMA takes a long time to construct, and I suspect that the extensive use of CMAs in science is a significant factor in their slower rate of course production. For the Arts Faculty the CMA has two disadvantages. It draws too rigid a line between factual knowledge and critical judgement. There must be few 'wrong' answers which *might* not be defended by a critical essay of pass or even distinction standard. I am a great disciple of Banesh Hoffmann's *The Tyranny of Testing*! And it's important that students in humanities shall not be led to think that there are absolute facts which are beyond challenge and above dispute. Further, we want our students to graduate as articulate in writing. We may overvalue this, though I do not think that we do. And we think that an essay every three weeks or so is the minimum for this end, and this leaves little resource for CMAs. So they form a small part of the foundation course in Arts and thereafter disappear. I suspect that we have not made sufficient use of them, probably more from a deep-seated mistrust of the machine than from any rational motive. At the other end of the scale, in advanced courses with smaller numbers, we are experimenting with lengthy projects or dissertations, occupying perhaps a quarter of the course, on topics agreed with the tutor. This will, we hope, encourage among other things genuine research on the local environment.

Because of the possibility of students receiving outside help, the University decided somewhat reluctantly that every course should be completed by a three-hour examination. This is a major administrative headache. Accommodation has to be found for 40,000 students all over the country over a comparatively short period. Because any combination of courses is possible, every course has to have two alternative papers so that students have a choice of times. (In the first year of a course the sweating academics have also to produce a specimen paper and a reserve paper—four papers in all covering the same ground.) There is a vast exercise of coordination, marking, monitoring and standardizing. The science-based courses use CMAs for some of their examination work also. In general the evaluation rests on human skill—or deficiency. If an examiner is found to be consistently lenient or severe he can be 'tagged'—singled out by a special symbol—and the information is available to the examining board for use in borderline cases. If the two papers seem from the results to be of a different standard (with large numbers this can readily be seen), it is possible for the computer to adjust the marks to an agreed mean, though this may create a fresh set of problems, since those who have been awarded a narrow pass-mark may thereby be failed and vice versa, but these borderline marks are awarded with great care, and the discrepancy is more likely to appear in the middle range.

The results of continuous assessment and of the examination are considered by an examining board, which invariably, even for foundation courses, contains external examiners. They will have received a selection of marked essays, across the year; they will have scrutinized and commented upon the question papers; and they will have received a cross-section of marked exam questions. At first the University took the line that continuous assessment was the thing and the examination was merely an extra check, but the official policy soon became that continuous assessment and examination would carry approximately equal weight. The examining board then is confronted with marks in each category, averaged by the computer, ranging (sometimes with subdivisions) from A (distinction) through B, C, D (narrow pass), F (fail) to R (bad fail). Some combinations are easy to assess: AA, at least in arts, is a clear distinction, DD must be a pass, however narrow, and any combination of Fs and Rs must fail. Others too are relatively easy: AC or CA becomes B, BD or DB becomes C, DR or RD becomes F. But some are very difficult, and here immense trouble is taken to scrutinize a representative selection of exam scripts in any one 'cell'; unfortunately, continuous assessment work is not available at the examiners' meeting.

For there is an obvious problem. The exam is there to test that the continuous assessment is the student's own work. But what does it tell you? If a candidate has an A or B on continuous assessment, and an F or R on the exam, is he a cheat or a bad examinee? For this reason the Academic Advisory Committee strongly suggested that at foundation level there should be a third form of assessment. Some faculties found this in work done at summer school, but there has been a growing sense that assessment at summer school was cutting right across the really important things happening there. Some faculties have used *viva voce* examinations in borderline cases. There are disadvantages in this. *Viva voce* tests are seldom satisfactory, and when a candidate knows at the outset that he is on the borderline he is unlikely to give of his best; they are also very time-consuming.

My own view is that we have not found the answer to assessment. Neither continuous assessment nor examination nor the combination nor any third form of assessment I know is satisfactory, and the whole system is inevitably cumbersome.

Each year's end is accompanied by a large number of representations from students explaining why they have not done as well as they should. Often these prove irrelevant: a student who has done perfectly well on continuous assessment and failed disastrously in the exam explains why he has not done better on continuous assessment. Generally, however painful it may be, we have to be hard-hearted. A man has changed his job and had to neglect his studies because of new responsibilities; we congratulate him, we understand his difficulties, but we cannot award him a credit for neglecting his studies, and he must show that he can master the course under more favourable auspices. Most of the letters, whether from students or counsellors, are absolutely genuine and troublous to read. But only in a small minority can we make allowances, and usually in these we require some kind of further test, *viva voce* or otherwise.

Evaluation of the foundation course is straightforward: distinction, pass or fail. But with all subsequent courses the student receives not merely a result related to that course (one of the strengths of the OU system is that a student who has partially completed a degree course has something to show for it: we laugh at the famous Indian qualification 'Failed B.A.', but it *is* a qualification, for it indicates considerable progress through the university) but one which may contribute to his eventual honours classification. So here his result will be Distinction, Pass 1, Pass 2 or Pass 3 corresponding roughly to the familiar first-class, upper second, lower second and third. His honours classification will be on his best four post-foundation-course credits, of which at least two must be post-second-level, post-second-level credits receiving a heavier weighting. The standard, of course, will be that of 'general honours' at other universities rather than special honours.

CHAPTER SIX

Students

The operation of admitting students began in 1970. What we did not know at all was what proportion of those offered places would accept, how many would take an initial look at their first course and then decide that it was not for them, and how many would 'drop out' or fail in the first year's work. I am afraid that the first question had not occurred to me as significant, but we have constantly had to 'top up' the number of offers made, because of refusals, and indeed now make offers on a scale 25 per cent higher than our agreed admissions figure. I had fused the other two questions together in my mind, but the University was surely wise in distinguishing them, and in allowing the initial process of registration as an OU student to take place in two stages, final registration being deferred until about Easter. The figure of those completing their registration at this period is the baseline for subsequent statistical calculations.

There is open admission; which is to say that there are no entrance qualifications, except (normally) the age of twenty-one, and certificates, diplomas and degrees are of no advantage or disadvantage to an applicant. An applicant who shows no signs of serious study at any point in his career may be advised by a counsellor to try his hand first at one of the gateway or preparatory courses provided by other institutions, but he is not bound to take the advice, and his application stands as good a chance as any other. We did, however, build into the selection procedure certain parameters (as we have learned to call them). The original four faculties were staffed on a roughly equal basis. There was more demand for the 'arts-based' courses; it was arguable that national need was stronger in the 'science-based' courses; it seemed sensible therefore that the original selection should show roughly equal numbers in all four faculties. After 1969 the applications leaned even more heavily towards the arts-based courses, and the proportions accepted had to be altered in their favour, though none of us was happy about this. The fact that Technology had a foundation course but Education did not, meant that the disproportion between the five courses in 1972 and 1973 was even larger. There are some encouraging signs of an increase in applicants for science-based courses; none the less, prospective students stand a far greater chance of being admitted in that area. This then is a parameter which has been used, and rightly.

Other parameters built into the system included the possibility of selection by region of the country. It would plainly have been wrong if a substantially higher proportion of our students came from the conurbations than the national average: after all they do have other opportunities for most activities. Equally, had we been overwhelmed by the isolated rural student it would have placed considerable strains on the system. In fact, we scarcely needed to apply this criterion: the number of applicants, and the result of a selection which was regionally random, gave a close approximation to the proportion of the total population in each region. Selection by profession, however, had to be used owing to the large number of teachers applying. I had certainly not envisaged the extraordinary demand for upgrading teaching qualifications to degrees. The situation was accentuated by the fact that one journal where free publicity was guaranteed was *The Times Educational Supplement*, and this is read principally by teachers, so that there was wider awareness among the teaching profession of our existence. It was arguable that this was the most important contribution we could possibly make to education, since better-qualified teachers meant better schooling. It was arguable also that to take large numbers of teachers ran counter to our purposes since they had had and taken their first chance. At any rate the numbers could not be allowed to get out of hand, though they tended to do so in the 'topping-up' procedure. In the event, in the first year about 37 per cent of our admissions were teachers; the figure has since fallen to under 30 per cent, and my personal feeling is that somewhere about 20 per cent would be right for a steady state. Other parameters which might have been used were those of age and sex. The majority of our students turn out to be in the 26-45 age-group, and about 40 per cent are aged between 26 and 35, but they range very widely and the oldest admitted has been an 81-year-old woman who remarked proudly that in six years' time she would be able to put B.A. after her name. Only 4 per cent of the original entry, however, were over 55. As to sex, those papers who scornfully decried us as the university of the middle-class housewife were far from the target. Housewives officially form 35 per cent of the population; in our initial intake they formed 10 per cent (this has included a delightfully constant figure of 0.1 per cent males), and no one knows whether they are or are not middle-class. I was myself expecting that we might have twice as many women as men, but the figures in the first year were the reverse of that, and only now are they beginning to approach equality.

When all this has been allowed for, actually or potentially, the selection has been done by computer on a 'first come, first served' basis. Even this principle has been under fire, and there are those who think that a random selection should be taken of all applicants at closing date. I do not myself share this. Unless the selection becomes so tight that those with better postal facilities are at a strong advantage, there is much to be said for admitting the people who are so keen that they make sure that their application is in early.

The total number of applications received for 1971 was 43,444. Of these some were invalid, and selection of the original 25,000 was made from 40,817. For 1972 the applicants numbered 34,222 in the final analysis, and the number of places available was 20,500. For 1973 the figures were: applicants 30,414, places 17,000. For 1974 the number of applicants rose again to 33,220, but the places fell to 15,000 owing to the high rate of success and persistence among existing students. The proportion of women in the first year was, as we have noticed, surprisingly small—only 30 per cent. It has risen steadily to 42.6 per cent.

The number of applicants accepted in 1971 was initially around 24,000. By the beginning of May and final registration it had stabilized at 20,000. None of us knew what proportion of these would succeed. In conventional American universities the drop-out rate in the freshman year is of the order of 50 per cent. None of us would have been gravely surprised had our figures been comparable. I do not think we would have been surprised, though we would have been disappointed, had our drop-out and failure rate been substantially higher. I do not think that any of us in our wildest dreams envisaged a pass-rate of 75 per cent in the first year. The Arts Faculty, predictably, had the highest percentage of passes, and the lowest percentage of distinctions, the Mathematics Faculty, equally predictably, the lowest percentage of passes and the highest percentage of distinctions. Most encouraging was the pass-rate in Science, which was over 70 per cent. In subsequent years the overall pass-rate has dropped slightly, as was to be expected, to about 70 per cent. It should be said that we resisted those who argued for a previously agreed percentage of passes. We thought we knew what academic standard we were seeking; there was no experience to suggest what proportion of our students would meet that standard. But the very success has caused problems. The government have fixed a plateau of 42,000 for our student population, not counting post-experience courses and postgraduate students. The greater our success-rate the fewer students we can admit in subsequent years. The numbers admitted had very quickly to be reduced to 15,000, and may have to be reduced even further. Our method of selection allows considerable flexibility here.

The number of applicants can be influenced, if not controlled, by the amount of resources put into publicity. It seems that for a satisfactory selection procedure we need about twice as many applicants as places, and therefore can cut off publicity at that point. Various forms of publicity have been tried; the most effective is undoubtedly a campaign in the *Radio Times*.

The commonest question in public discussion of the Open University is 'Are you satisfied with the proportion of working-class applicants?' To this there can be only one answer: 'No!' None the less, *tout court*, it is a misleading answer. For, in the first place, by anybody's standards something of the order of 15 per cent of our intake of students come from among manual workers, industrial and factory workers, farm-workers, post-office workers, bus-drivers, taxi-drivers and the like. The exact figure is difficult to determine, and the 15 per cent figure comes from the students' evaluation of themselves; market research classification would put it lower (but that includes income); I should myself put it marginally higher. This is a relatively small proportion of the total student population. But in absolute figures it means over 5,000 people. Anyone who suddenly sets up a university for 5,000 manual workers would be regarded as achieving a minor miracle, even if that university were performing no other function at all. In the second place, we could undoubtedly increase the enrolment from among manual workers if we put more resources into advertisement in that area. But the Information Officer is working with a limited budget, and has to husband his resources jealously, and use them cost-effectively. The educational correspondents of *The Times*, the *Guardian* and the *Daily Telegraph* give excellent coverage to Open University matters; their readers are well aware of the University and its potential for them. An advertisement in those will bring an immediate response. Readers of the *Daily Mail*, the *Daily Mirror* and the *News of the World* have often not heard of the Open University and an advertisement there would pass them by. It is my view that growth in this area will be inescapably slow, and will depend very much on propaganda carried out by those manual workers already in the system. But there may be imaginative and inexpensive approaches which might spark off something—a stall at the Cup Final, a letter to the Old Codgers and the like. And we hope that the accession of Victor, now Lord, Feather to the University Council will lead to an increased support among Trades Unionists.

Thirdly, however, it is not true that the Open University is a middle-class organization in the obvious sense. The majority of our students came from working-class homes, and if they were applying for one of the other universities, they would be classified as working-class, for these classifications depend on the profession of the parent, not of the applicant. A typical and illuminating example is a police-inspector with whom we were discussing this very point. He said: 'I'm a police-inspector. You might think therefore I was middle-class. But I'm not. I'm working-class born and bred. I left school at 15. I worked my way up from the beat by sheer hard work. And I want the education commensurate with the job I'm doing.' The vast majority of our teachers went to training-colleges or colleges of education because they were in some way deprived: perhaps their parents could afford only two years before they started earning an income, or perhaps they had been to a poor school which never set their minds aflame or simply didn't have the teachers competent to help them to achieve university entrance. In other words the majority of our students have been partially but not totally deprived. They have had an opening and an opportunity, but not as large an opening or as rich an opportunity as their capacities warranted. They have had half a chance; the Open University is for them the university of the one-and-a-halfth chance.

Let us look at a few students. Here is a man in his middle-forties who grew up in South Wales, left school at fourteen and went into Ebbw Vale Steelworks. Gradually he came to play an increasing part in the life of the community until he became branch secretary of the Transport and General Workers' Union. He takes his responsibilities seriously, and has been a regular attender at Workers' Educational Association classes, but they could not provide for him the opportunity the OU has done. He is not interested in the qualification so much as in the education. Here is a woman in her fifties, who had always yearned to work in mathematics, but who had been to a school where the teaching in this area was depressingly bad. But she always remembered her headmistress saying 'Sylvia, it's never too late to learn', and now the chance to learn has come. Here is a Scot from a working-class home who had to leave school at sixteen when his father's health broke down. He became a trouble-shooter for the old Highland Railway, always on the move, but always eager to learn and to serve. He became a magistrate and Provost of his home town—and now at sixty-three has the chance taken from him at sixteen. Here is the daughter of a publican, who left school at sixteen because her father couldn't afford university for her. She became an assistant computer analyst and married an aircraft engineer. 'I always felt I was missing out,' she said, 'and this seems to be a perfect solution because you can work in your own home, at your own time and at your own pace.' Here is a parson, who frankly admits that the Latin-qualification demanded in his day by other universities scared him off. This is his second chance; he wants it to acquire a better understanding of his fellow men. Here is a 35-year-old marine engineer, who left school at fifteen after attending fourteen different schools, and now wants a proper training in mathematics and science. Here is a 68-year-old; in his day university education was still for the privileged few, but all his daughters have been to college, and he, a man of sensitive intelligence, wants 'to follow in his daughters' footsteps'. Here is a 29-year-old salesman, who feels he must get out of the rut of his present job, and wants to see what he can do in scientific studies. I think most of us regretted that Clive Lloyd, the West Indian cricketer, applied too late to get admission; the admission of Miss Keep Fit for 1972 was a partial compensation.

Or look for a moment at a group of eight students in one of the top-security prisons. 'Up to now', writes a tutor, 'their lives have been of uniform drab monotony, only varied by terrifying outbursts of violence.' 'Obviously', she goes on, 'the OU course can't change everything overnight for them; but I wish you could see what it *has* done for them. Their minds, thirsting for knowledge, are soaking it up like rain in a desert; and although the desert is still full of bristling cacti—which prickle with a vengeance on occasion!—it is also putting out vigorous healthy shoots in all directions.' She has a fascinating account of the different effect of various parts of the Arts foundation course upon them. Some find release through art; prison seems to heighten the imagination, and particularly the sense of colour. Others have valued the music, though the technical aspects have been a stumbling-block. There is little experience of literature, and this makes poetry difficult, but it also leaves them unexpectedly open, for instance to Kafka. There was a strong sense of self-identification with the downtrodden Gregor in his horrific short story 'Metamorphosis'. Socrates proved a revelation to them and offered a therapeutic experience, for they identified themselves with Socrates in prison, yet saw that he had something they lacked. Something similar happened for some of them over involvement with Jesus in 'What is a Gospel?' though any inclination to sanctimoniousness meets with considerable hostility. An exceptionally valuable experience involved bringing students from outside to share in a joint seminar. Two of the prison students and two of the others read papers. Apart from the value of contact with the outside world, there was the knowledge that they could hold their own in serious conversation and serious study. 'All these men', writes the tutor, 'are experiencing a kind of Renaissance within themselves.' If only a few can have a sustaining purpose to keep them going during their remaining years in prison, if only a few can leave with a degree and the possibility of constructive work, the whole thing will have been amply justified. Altogether there were thirty-five enrolled prisoners in the first year, and thirty passed, an encouraging rate. By 1974 the number had risen to forty-six; they were not, however, allowed to do science because of the dangerous nature of some of the experimental material. It was accounted newsworthy in both *The Times* and the *Daily Mirror* that one of the first women admitted was Myra Hindley, in the public eye for her association with a murder which hit the headlines; it is excellent to think of this as part of her rehabilitation.

Handicapped students provide the University with one of its greatest challenges—and opportunities. In 1973 nearly 400 disabled students attended summer schools. Dr Vida Carver has been chairman of a coordinating committee to help disabled students. The Open University is, for example, the first university to provide special facilities for deaf students, although more children are deaf than blind. Plainly there are parts of the courses, music for example, which are largely inaccessible to the deaf student, though even in music some intelligent understanding remains possible, for music and mathematics are not far away from one another. The Open University depends less on presentation through the spoken word than most universities, but in radio and television, and especially in summer school, dependence on this form of communication is important. Dr Carver's committee has developed four principal ways of helping deaf students through the aural parts of their course. First there is the concept of pairing: a deaf student is paired with a volunteer who will give him a transcript or summary of broadcast programmes. This is not so easily operable in the complexities of summer school. But summer schools make other resources possible. So second, we have the resources of modern technology and the use of an induction coil to pick up a lecturer's voice carried from a neck microphone on a loop of wire; this method, incidentally, is readily adaptable to radio and TV listening. Thirdly, the Royal National Institute for the Deaf has lent the University a machine for the translation of speech into visual display. The machine requires a highly skilled operator, and cannot as yet keep pace with a lecturer, so that the system involves a paraphrase of the lecture for the keyboard operator, but Gerald Hales, the Open University's research officer in this field, is hoping to develop the system. Fourthly, Phil Bobbins, an expert in sign language, has been providing simultaneous translation of lectures and seminars for deaf students. It can be hard work, for metaphysical ideas may not easily be rendered in sign language. The approach is thus flexible. One important aspect of it is that it pays off at compound interest, so to speak. There is a double handicap in deafness, the physical inability to hear, and the mental and emotional strain arising from that inability. Phil Bobbins has said finely: 'The aim is to take some of the stress out of the learning process. The effort channelled out of the process can be spent learning more.'

Blind students have received enormous help from the Royal

National Institute for the Blind. Again, there are parts of the courses which may be largely inaccessible to them, some aspects of design or art history for instance, though we may remember Locke's friend, blind from birth, who when asked what the word 'scarlet' conveyed to him, replied 'The sound of a trumpet'. Even that superb answer makes the point: for the deaf, the audible must be conveyed visually; for the blind, the visual must be conveyed audibly. So the basic help for blind students is the translation of the written word either into Braille, or more generally on to tape which can be listened to. It is a large undertaking, and the Institute has done remarkable work. Vida Carver has hopes, however, that the system of pairing, developed for deaf students, may prove equally applicable to the blind, and so relieve some of the pressures.

Students are required to take two foundation courses. The great majority opt for two science-based courses or two arts-based courses. There are a hundred or so each year in each of the other combinations, and this is good. But we have not really succeeded in bridging Sir Charles Snow's Two Cultures. There are encouraging signs, however, that the right interfaculty courses lead to a warm response. The most successful of all these is the second-level course *The Biological Bases of Behaviour* which has attracted students both from S100 and from D100. Another important contribution is in the History of Science courses. The first, *Science and the Rise of Technology since 1800*, predictably attracted those who had taken the combination of S100 and A100, but also proved of interest to students whose main interests lay in Science and Technology. The second, *Science and Belief from Copernicus to Darwin*, was deliberately slanted to prove more attractive to those who think of themselves as arts students, and has on the whole succeeded in this.

The student profile is complicated by the Credit Exemptions system. It was from an early stage part of the vision of the Open University that we might pioneer in a more flexible higher education system whereby students might be able to transfer from one institution to another. Our first contribution to this lay through a system of credit exemptions. The principle behind this is that an applicant who has studied at a university level might have one credit exemption for each year of study successfully completed at university level, up to three. Thus the holder of a degree would indubitably be entitled to three credit exemptions, and a university student who had successfully passed all hurdles except the last, would be entitled to two. But there are many other equivalences far less clear, and the Credit Exemptions Committee is one of the hardest working of all University committees. By 1973 no less than 35,000 students had been awarded credit exemptions. It was natural that there would be exemptions from one foundation course, but the University properly insisted that all students should do one foundation course, or they might miss the very basis of our approach. The University has been set by the ears by one early decision. This was that colleges of education should be deemed equivalent in standard to universities, and that those with a two-year teaching qualification should be entitled to two credit exemptions, those with a three-year teaching qualification to three. The decision was made and announced. It was subsequently hotly challenged by some members of Senate, who felt that the way was being unduly smoothed for teachers. The guarantee had been given, and could not honourably be withdrawn. The original decision was that no student at all was entitled to a third credit exemption except in a defined area. This limitation was withdrawn for all except teachers. This meant that for teachers, instead of being general and absolute, the exemption was made conditional on their concentrating on courses in the Education Faculty. It was an odd compromise, and largely unsatisfactory. On the face of it, it would seem that these, however invigorating, were the very courses to which they ought not to be directed, and they ought rather to be encouraged to deepen their expertise in their teaching subjects.

More recently the James Report on Teacher Education and Training and the development of the Diploma in Higher Education has led to a further reappraisal, the results of which are not yet firm. The University is in a difficult situation precisely because of the pioneering steps we have taken. If we recognize the Dip.H.E. as enabling students to complete a degree with one further year's work of university standard (i.e. two of our credits), we are excusing the holders of the diploma from four credits, while we excuse holders of a degree from only three. If we do not, we may be out-of-step with other universities. Initial thinking in the Credit Exemptions Committee favours accepting the anomaly and receiving a credit *transfer* system and a credit *exemptions* system side by side; but it's no use pretending that it isn't anomalous.

The credit exemptions system gave a fine opportunity for those who accuse us scornfully of being too middle-class to point their finger at our first graduation ceremony. Of course the majority of the graduates at that ceremony were in some sense middle-class. They could not have graduated in two years unless they had at least two credit exemptions, that is, unless they had already had the opportunity of at least two years of higher education. They are by no means a representative profile of the total student body.

Some comparative figures for new entries to foundation courses may be useful:

	1971	*1972*	*1973*	*1974* (approx)
A100	6,112	5,732	3,635	4,132
D100	6,001	6,720	4,296	4,677
M100	4,639	4,159	1,822	2,000
S100	4,963	4,001	2,057	2,333
T100	—	1,649	1,337	2,244
TOTAL	21,715	22,261	13,147	15,38

Initially quite a number of students attempted two foundation courses in the same year. This was a heavy load, and by 1973 it had dropped to 742 or not more than about 6 per cent of the whole. One interesting aspect of the foundation courses is the number of teachers who opt for D100. Of the ongoing courses those in education were the most heavily subscribed. This is partly but not wholly explained by the credit exemptions system, and about a third of the students in education courses come from outside the teaching profession. All their second-level courses attracted over 2,000 students and *Personality Growth and Learning* actually topped the 3,000. The only other courses with comparable figures were the two second-level courses in Arts, both around the 2,000 mark, though special mention should be made of two interfaculty courses, *Biological Bases of Behaviour* and *Science and the Rise of Technology since 1800*, both of which topped the 1,200 mark. In general the staying-power of students is impressive, and, once final registration is complete, it is exceptional for the students 'live on file' to fall below 90 per cent of those finally registered. Women have tougher staying-power than men. Not all of these, however, will take the examination, and it has been calculated that about 25 per cent of all the students do not seem seriously interested in taking a degree or in receiving qualifications at all, but are simply interested in the courses for their own sakes. More credit to them.

Statistics for 1971 are not fully adequate, but it may be of interest to have the proportions of the members of different occupational groups to whom offers were made in the three subsequent years:

	1972	*1973*	*1974* (approx)
Housewives	10.6 (2,290)	12.4 (2,636)	13.3 (488)
Armed Forces	1.9 (397)	2.3 (482)	2.6 (2,110)
Managerial	4.7 (999)	4.3 (908)	3.8 (615)
Education	29.9 (6,306)	28.6 (6,130)	29.1 (4,628)
Professions	12.5 (2,630)	11.4 (2,417)	10.8 (1,712)
Scientists	4.8 (1,009)	4.2 (885)	3.9 (623)
Technicians	12.1 (2,555)	13.1 (2,796)	12.7 (2,051)
Electrical	3.2 (681)	3.4 (738)	3.2 (498)
Manufacturing	2.3 (491)	2.2 (471)	2.2 (348)
Transport	1.3 (280)	1.6 (336)	1.6 (247)
Clerical	9.7 (1,881)	8.8 (1,890)	9.1 (1,453)
'Services'	4.2 (895)	4.3 (906)	3.9 (620)
'Not working'	3.0 (647)	3.1 (671)	3.6 (564)
In institutions	0.1 (24)	0.2 (40)	0.2 (37)
TOTAL	100.5 (21,085)	100.0 (21,306)	100.0 (15,994)

The 100.5 per cent is no doubt an eccentricity of the computer. The categories are mostly self-explanatory but 'services' is a bit of a ragbag including hotel proprietors and chimney sweeps, auctioneers and waitresses, commercial travellers and the fire brigade, models and barmen. The proportion of offers seldom varies more than 1 per cent from the proportion of applicants; the only striking divergence is in the case of technicians, who formed 11.2 per cent of the 1973 applicants and 9.8 per cent of those in 1974, but received 13.1 and 12.7 per cent of the offers. Plainly, some occupational groups favour some courses rather than others: thus the housewives formed 22.3 per cent of all the applicants for A100 and only 2.2 per cent of those for T100, whereas the technicians formed 3.4 per cent of Arts applicants and 32.6 per cent of Technology applicants. Those from the armed forces show a significantly higher interest in science-

based subjects. Still, such relative figures may obscure important facts: 450 technicians asking for a course in arts and 55 housewives asking for a course in technology are not negligible.

In 1972, 8.6 per cent of students provisionally registered had no formal qualifications at all, and as many as 32.8 per cent had not progressed beyond O-level in the General Certificate of Education; at the other end, 5.3 per cent were university graduates.

The overall pass-rate continues to run at about 70 per cent for most courses. This is on the face of it satisfactory, until it is realized that mathematically this would mean, ignoring credit exemptions and resits, a graduation rate of about 12 per cent after six credits. Even that would not be wholly disreputable, representing as it would about 2,000 graduates a year. But it would be disappointingly low. Fortunately the outlook is brighter, since the pass-rate is depressed by those who are not interested in the examination. My own uninformed guess would be that somewhere around 50 per cent of our students will end up with degrees.

As would be expected, students with qualifications do in fact do better than those without. If you compare those gaining credits in foundation courses in 1972, and compare the pass-rate for those in the teaching profession with those who have not progressed beyond O-levels and may not have progressed as far, in M100 it is three times as high, in S100 twice as high, and in the others, about half as high again (the success of the unqualified student in technology compared with the other science-based courses is notable). At second level the disparity continued but followed a less predictable pattern. It was heaviest in MST281 (*Elementary Mathematics for Science and Technology*, a substitute foundation course). It was high also in MST282 (*Mechanics and Applied Calculus*) and, curiously, in D281 (*New Trends in Geography*). In the sciences it was highest in chemistry, lowest in biology. It was extremely low in *Linear Mathematics* and lowest of all in *Decision-making in Britain*. But only in the two arts courses did more than half of those without any qualification at all obtain a credit.

A word about postgraduate students. The University has moved cautiously in this area. In 1971 there were 30 registered, in 1972 100, in 1973 204; the total is expected to reach 350 by 1976. Of those presently registered, 40 are in Arts, 37 in Education, 38 in Science, 27 in Social Science, 28 in Technology, 15 in Mathematics, and 19 under the IET (Institute of Educational Technology). The University offers a B.Phil., M.Phil., and Ph.D., representing the equivalent of one, two or three years' full-time work respectively, together with the attainment of an appropriate standard of research. Postgraduate students are not at present supplied with course-material or broadcasts, though this may come. Some of them are supervised by central academics; these include some research assistants and course assistants. Others, more remote, may be required to find a supervisor accessible to them and acceptable to the University. The supervisor will award credits, one for the equivalent of a term's work; a student may not submit his dissertation until he has accumulated the requisite three, six or nine credits. The fees range from £110 to £290. The University has been cautiously conventional in scrutinizing the qualifications for admission to postgraduate study. Here we are not open, and sooner or later we shall have to be more enterprising. We have also made what seems a misguided decision to admit no student unless there is a full-time academic expert in his field of research upon the University staff. In view of the limited size of our staff this seems an intolerable restriction on student choice, and the quality of the external supervisors (most of them of the staff of other universities), and a stringent system of external examiners, should be enough to guarantee standards. Still, we have made a beginning, and the first graduation ceremony saw the award of two Ph.Ds, one in mathematics and one in history.

Finally, to return briefly to the ordinary undergraduates. They have had a deal of social adjustment to make. For some of them it has been the end of their former social life, which was undoubtedly sometimes, but by no means always, empty. Evening and weekend study has made inroads upon past activities. But for some it has been not merely the opening of new windows in the mind of the individual, but the start of a new or richer social life linked with the things of the mind. Some study centres have become in a real sense friendship centres; and for some, whose lives had been dominated by home or job, they have been a liberation. The Rev. Lloyd Caddick, Rector of Bulwick, and himself a tutor and counsellor, and a member of the University Council, is proud to have married two students who met one another at his study centre, Susan Dodsworth and Michael Askew; the newspapers carried such headlines as LOVE WAS NO MERE ACADEMIC MATTER FOR THEM. Summer schools have been the beginning of new friendships, and have brought together unexpected people; there are not many places where you will find a peeress and a coalminer chatting entirely naturally about their common work. Of course, Open University work has sometimes put strains on family life, and the chief comment of one of the first graduates was 'students need sympathetic families'. Where the husband or wife does not understand or sympathize with the other's dedication to study, it can put a serious strain upon a marriage. But others have found that it has enriched their family life. I think of some families where husband and wife are both students, and their intellectual interaction with one another in consequence. I think of the tolerant amusement of some children, one of whom remarked 'Mummy, that university is sending you silly. All you say is "uum",' and another of whom looks forward to the arrival of philosophy units illustrated by cartoons so that she can look at 'Mummy's comic strip'. I think of a mother whose daughter left school without a needed A-level in English. The daughter was shy about going to evening classes on her own, so her mother, a delightful extrovert, bubbling over with joy, said 'I'll come along with you, ducks; it'll be a bit of fun.' The daughter got her grade E pass; the mother got an A and thought 'What a lark! What about this Open University thing?' and is now with the admiration and enthusiasm of her family delightedly moving through a degree programme with excellent grades. And I think of a woman with seven children under 12, whose Open University work has made a united family still more united, and whose husband, whose parents and whose husband's parents have all been sharing in the care of the children during her summer schools and other absences.

Three comments from students may round off this picture. The first from a police-constable: 'The work is exhilarating, but also exhausting.' The second from a housewife: 'Knowledge is so much of life.' The third from a secretary: 'It messes up your whole life—but it's worth it.'

CHAPTER SEVEN

Organization Man

Naomi McIntosh, when Senior Lecturer in Research Methods, said that the University 'resembles at some stages a production plant rather than an academic institution'. 'It's the numbers that numb', said Michael Drake in the early days as Acting Dean of Social Science, 'some 22,000 applicants; nearly 8,000 enrolments; 85,000 essays to mark; 64,000 assignments for the computer; 24 summer schools in five different universities from Exeter in the south to Stirling in the north; almost 300 study centres; over 1,000 part-time tutors—and that's just for one course.' The scale of operations *is* enormous. In 1971 students did about 160,000 TMAs and 160,000 CMAs. In 1972 they did 243,537 TMAs and 258,417 CMAs. The figures for 1973 are not available, but they will surely not be far from the 300,000 mark for each. This means that in a given year there are already more than half a million exercises passing to and fro between student and tutor or computer, and across three years there have been not far off a million and a half in all. Each year the University sends out some 2.7 million routine mailings to students. The Phillipsburg packaging machine, with its nine stations for incorporating different materials into the envelope, is, or was, the largest in Europe. By 1974 these mailings will have included not much under 5,000 different teaching documents. The recipients for each mailing are recorded by the computer, which prints out the appropriate set of names and addresses. In addition there are 33,000 mailings of home-experiment kits a year, and 1,000 packing cases sent out as part of the summer-school operation, including anything from special books to wheelchairs for disabled students. The University's postal bill is of the order of £200,000 a year with an additional cost of £34,000 a year for material despatched through British

Road Services. Warehousing at present covers 55,000 square feet, and the operations area employs 212 people.

The University consumes an extraordinary quantity of paper. One Senate meeting in 1972 meant the circulation of 272 sheets of paper to each member of Senate. This added up to well over 100,000 sheets in all. Each member of Senate received paper weighing 2lbs 8ozs. And there are four statutory meetings of Senate each year. In 1972 the University used 400 reams of A4 paper each week; in 1973 it was more like 600 reams. In 1972 the reprographic services, one of the hardest-working parts of a hard-working university, made 19 million 'impressions'; in 1973 the figure was about 25 million.

An operation of this size would be impossible without the use of a computer. I have already indicated something of the work of the computer. The figure shows something of how the work looked in the second half of 1973. It may be helpful to spell out one or two aspects of the work more fully. For example, the Admissions system has three main aspects—application, allocation and acceptance. The first involves processing applications as received, and analysing them periodically; each applicant receives a computer-printed acknowledgement. Allocation involves applying any parameters agreed in the light of the analysis of applicants; the exercise results in a division between those accepted, those reserve-listed, and those rejected. Acceptance involves the despatch of computer-printed letters to all applicants, with a request for fees, and 'topping-up' from the reserve list to replace those who either decline or do not send the money.

The file of those who accept is merged with student records. The maintenance and updating of the file is one of the more complex businesses; change of address is only one of some thirty changes which may be recorded. Requests for fees are computer-printed; fees are paid in through the bank Giro system, and the bank from time to time supplies magnetic tapes so that the details may be recorded. Students are asked during the course of the year to give in order of preference the courses they would wish to take in the following year (*a*) if they are successful (*b*) if they are not. This information is stored and can be extracted as a guide to planning. When the results are known the computer makes the allocation in the light of the results, the expressed preferences of students, and course-guides. (A course with a home-experiment kit has an upper limit.) Throughout the year the

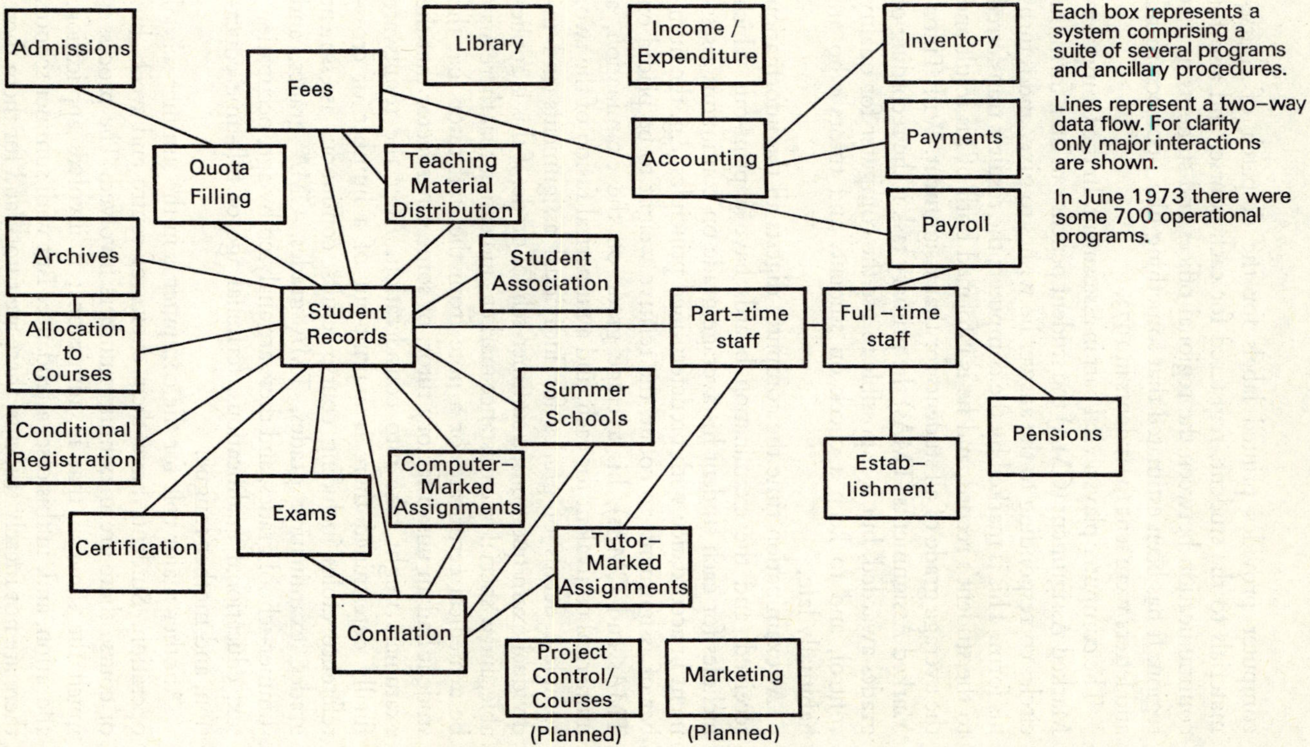

FIG. 4 Open University integrated computer systems for management of the educational process

computer provides printed labels for the despatch of course-materials to the students registered for each course, and also for communication between the regional offices and students in that region. It has been estimated that something like 1,000,000 forms and letters were sent to students in 1973.

The computer plays a vital part in assessment. In the Computer-Marked Assignment (CMA) the student pencils out on a form the circles corresponding to the answer he wishes to give, and returns his form. This is marked by the computer; the result is transferred to the student's record, and he is informed both of his result and the average grade of all students for that assignment. With Tutor-Marked Assignments (TMAs) the primary task is the recording of grades awarded, but it is possible to use the computer for quality control, and to keep a check on students and tutors who are habitually late.

At examination time the computer digests all the information received, and the examination boards have a print-out which includes for each student his average grade on continuous assessment in accordance with predetermined principles (e.g. the number of assignments to count, the relative weight to be placed on TMAs and CMAs), his average grade on the examination, a numerical equivalent for each, and a numerical fusion of the two, complete details of grades for individual assignments and individual exam questions, a summer-school grade, if this is applicable, and a 'special circumstance marker', indicating that there may be a medical certificate, or a note from the staff tutor that the student had an unsatisfactory tutor, or some other factor that the examiners might take into consideration. After the results are finally determined there is a print-out of a number of cross-reference tables including course results, continuous assessment grades, examination grades, TMA grades, CMA grades, and summer-school grades, and these are analysed by age, occupation, sex, educational qualifications, terminal age of full-time education, and mother tongue.

Another major role for the computer is in the summer-school operation. Students have their choice of centre and week, but of course there are maximum numbers involved. The process is much the same as that in admissions; it involves application, allocation, and, in this case, attendance. But with summer schools there are not merely students, there are tutors, and for them there has to be a selection procedure. This involves some prior information. Applications once received are referred by region to the staff tutors, who classify them roughly as *Yes*, *Perhaps*, and *No*. Most of them will be already known as course-tutors; it usually, though not quite invariably, follows that a good course-tutor will be a good summer-school tutor. They are also scrutinized by the central academics, who will know those who have served in previous years, and who can also give a judgement on applications from academics who are not course-tutors. With this information, together with the stated preferences of applicants, the computer can distribute the tutors appropriately.

All this is only a fraction of the work of the computer, which has many more routine functions, for example in maintaining the records and controlling the payment both of the full-time and of the part-time staff, or in providing the University with an integrated accounting system. In the middle of 1973 there were altogether no less than 700 operational programs.

The present computer is an ICL 1903T computer offering 96K core of storage, a 600-card-per-minute reader, a fast line printer printing at 1,350 lines per minute, a document-reader reading 5,000 documents per hour (for CMAs), 4 disk transports with 60 million characters of storage each, and 6 × 60Kc/s magnetic tape transports. In 1975 we hope to move over to a Univac 1106 processor offering 131K of storage, a 9300 slave processor with 12,000 bytes of memory and 600-card-per-minute reader attached, a 1,400 line-per-minute printer, 6 disk packs with a capacity of 43 million characters each, and 4,016 magnetic tape units transferring at a rate of 192,000 characters per second, together with the ICL document-reader.

Such a mass organization means that if anything goes wrong it goes massively wrong. At the end of his first year Student A00327756 wrote to the *Daily Telegraph* about some of his experiences. Misprints were one problem. A Stop Press notice, referring to a diagram on population ratios in a city and running 'You should note that on D100 S32 SA page 10 of 23 pages Pyramid D has been printed upside down and reversed left to right' created nearly as many problems as the original. The omission of 'not' in a logic exercise was particularly unfortunate; another error in a logic passage drew the esoteric correction 'The translation of "you can have sausages or fish fingers" requires & and not v.' Mistakes in computer-marked assignments are particularly difficult to cope with, for the computer simply does not understand. Sometimes there seems no way out. An overzealous member from the operations area took a CMA from an office without authority. It was in draft only and did not match the computer's instructions. In consequence all students were given R, a bad failure. This created a storm of protest. Students were promised that the grade would be ignored. But this did not meet the case. Some were ashamed to have even an ignored R on their record; yet to alter it was a major operation. Others did not like losing what might have been a good mark in their strong area.

Student A00327756 is particularly hard on the computer, not without some justification. He draws attention to a notorious incident when the computer erroneously expelled some 600 students for alleged non-payment of fees. He also notes its occasional unwarranted generosity in awarding unearned As, 'errors unfortunately spotted later on'. But it is the impersonality, inhumanity and inflexibility of the computer which arouses his greatest fears. Some students did not have their registration recorded. It took some months to correct the error, but during that time they received no teaching materials and had no work corrected. As far as the computer was concerned, they did not exist. Tutors also have been lost in the system, and have remained unpaid for months on end. Such lost souls are officially termed 'unstructured' or 'randomized'.

'Meanwhile,' he concludes, 'let employers take note—anyone with a B.A. (Open) will not only have reached a good academic standard but will have undergone rigorous character-training in overcoming disasters and coping with difficulties. At any rate, I and thousands more are sufficiently impressed to go forward for another year. Provided, of course, that we are not unstructured or randomized by that blasted computer.'

Another who felt strongly his position as 'organization man' was B0075488, who claimed to be depersonalized with a nationality of 771, a mother tongue 144, occupations 05 and 12 (with 01 on the side), educational level L, and to have last studied at 9 where he read 10. Good clean fun—but it points to a real danger. With an operation as large as the Open University, administrative records are more accurately, efficiently, economically and expeditiously carried out by computer. But it is equally efficient in error. And because a computer inevitably depersonalizes, it is important that other aspects of our Brave New World should be as personal as possible. For Miranda's new world was brave only because of the people in it.

The world implications of the Open University made themselves clear early. One of the first universities to respond was the technological university at Benin in Nigeria. They were interested in using the foundation-course science material in their own face-to-face teaching situation, and in fact purchased 50 home-experiment kits, a complete set of broadcast tapes, and 100 copies of the correspondence texts. In general, the marketing operation has been a considerable success. In 1971 upwards of 75,000 individual books were sold to the general public, libraries or institutions; this was, of course, for the first four foundation courses only. (A book is a single unit or a number of units under one cover.) In 1972, with more courses available, the sales more than doubled. By 31 July the 1973 figures had soared to about 325,000, giving total figures of well over half a million. In the first year M100 sold best in total, but D100 (*Understanding Society*) with fewer volumes had the best average sale. By 1973 A100 had outstripped the others both in total and in average sales, with S100 next of the foundation courses; second-level material in the social sciences, geography, economics and sociology, had also sold particularly well, as had a rearrangement of material from the Maths foundation course in textbook form. Films and audio-tapes naturally could not show quite such astronomical figures, but in the two and a half years from January 1971, sales were about 2,861 and 4,070 respectively; the figures for 1973 alone were up to 2,729 films and 5,683 audio-tapes by December.

The marketing side is developing strongly in North America. 'Not since one millionaire purchased entire Scottish castles and had them shipped here stone by stone', wrote Norman Birnbaum (Tunstall 37), 'has there been such crass cultural transfer.' Late in 1972 an agreement was reached by which Harper and Row, the well-known New York publishers, became official publishing representatives of the University in North America with exclusive rights for the sale and distribution of textbooks, films and audio-tapes. Anthony Mellor, representing Harper and Row, said at the time that this was 'the most important new venture we have undertaken in the field of post-secondary education'. 'The Open University's integrated teaching system', he added, 'has great attractions for American colleges, particularly at a time when the adult education programme is being expanded with Federal

Government support while at the same time the rising costs of traditional forms of university education are creating severe financial problems for both colleges and state governments.' The initial order, covering the original four foundation courses only, had a list price of $500,000, but it was expected that across the first four years sales would top the $5,000,000 and might rise much higher: the expansion in North America has resulted in the opening of a North American office.

American universities did in fact embark upon pilot experiments with Open University material. These were Rutgers, Maryland and Houston; one interesting aspect has been the variously charming and impressive quality of the women in charge of the scheme. One curious feature of these American experiments was the uselessness of radio programmes in the US; Americans are not accustomed to listening to serious radio talks. The potential in America is undoubtedly very great. Apart from the points noted above, there is the immense challenge of Latin America, and it is with an eye for adaptation there that Houston is conducting its pilot experiment. The vast tracts of some of the states and some of the provinces of Canada offer scope for Open University methods. But even in the conventional situation our courses offer better teaching and higher academic standards than are to be found in many Liberal Arts Colleges.

The major world potential of the Open University is not, except for a very temporary period, the direct use of our materials by other countries. The Third World does not want a study of humanities, or sociology, which is focused on Britain, but on their own scene. Their biology must be related to their own plants and animals. Even their mathematics must draw its illuminating illustrations from the local scene. If the Third World is to develop its own Open University, it must produce its own courses. What we can offer is not the finished product but the knowhow. We can offer consultancy services. They will inevitably not be cheap. A skilled and experienced man away for an extended period will not be replaced adequately by another at the same salary. It will take two, three or even four inexperienced people to begin to cover the work he would have done. But the potential is enormous. We have glimpsed it in the Ministers of Education from all over the world who have come to Walton Hall. And it is a contribution we will gladly make to others who have not had a first chance of university education, let alone a second.

The Open University would never have been founded had it not been cost-effective. This was one of the points made by Eurich and Schwenkmeyer of the Academy for Educational Development Inc. Writing in the summer of 1971, they drew attention to the fact that at the point when students began their courses the University had spent about £2 million of the amount budgeted for development. To establish an ordinary university of only 5,000 students would have cost something like six times that sum. Leslie Wagner in an important article in *Higher Education* in 1972 gave some revealing figures about running costs. At that date the average recurrent cost per equivalent undergraduate was £251 in the OU and £940 in conventional universities. The capital cost per student place is £165 as compared with £3,000. What this means is that the drop-out rate would have to reach 85 per cent before the cost of producing a graduate in the OU equalled that of conventional universities. But even these figures are misleading. For a substantial proportion of undergraduates at residential universities have their board and lodging paid for at public expense, whereas our own students are home-based. Further, in the ordinary university system students are for the most part economically non-productive, while Open University students are generally in full employment and contributing to the GNP; Wagner has calculated that the difference might amount to £30 million per annum.

How much does it cost a student to graduate? He pays £10 for provisional registration, and £15 tuition fee for each foundation course. The fee for each course beyond the foundation level is £25. His basic tuition fee for six full credits therefore adds up to £140 in all. If he takes half-credit courses it will rise slightly but not much. In addition he will have to pay £37 for each summer school he attends. This adds a further £74 for his two foundation courses, though local education authorities have in general met this cost. If he is in the science-based area his costs here will be heavier. He will also have to buy a certain number of books. For foundation courses the provision has been held to £10, for later courses normally to £15, though with rising costs we shall not be able to hold these maxima for long. This adds a further £80, but he has the books at the end. In science-based subjects he has to pay a deposit on his home-experiment kit, but that is returnable. And of course he requires access to a radio, TV set, and for some courses a record player. But assuming he has access to these, the necessary outlay is less than £300 for a degree, and less than £400 for an honours degree.

How are decisions to be taken in such a vast organization? The structure is naturally not essentially different from that of other universities. The governing body is the Council. The Council is charged by the Charter with 'advancing the interests of the University, maintaining its efficiency, encouraging teaching, the pursuit of learning and the prosecution of research therein'. The Council consists of the University Officers (Chancellor, Pro-Chancellor, Vice-Chancellor and Treasurer), the Chairman of the Academic Advisory Committee, four members appointed by the Privy Council, three members appointed by the Committee of Vice-Chancellors and Principals, three members representative of local education authorities and one of education authorities in Scotland, one member appointed by the Royal Society, one member appointed by the BBC, the Pro-Vice-Chancellors, six members appointed by the Senate, two representatives of the part-time teaching staff and two of the students, and a few coopted members. The University Secretary is naturally Secretary to the Council. The Council is thus a weighty and distinguished body. It meets at intervals of approximately two months, and attendance is good; members are proud to be associated with the OU, and several of its members give generously of their time to sit on other University boards and committees. The Council has the ultimate responsibility for the conduct of all University affairs, and particular responsibility for financial matters.

Senate is jealous of its rights (which are scrupulously observed by the Council) in academic matters. But there are few academic decisions which do not cost money, and few financial decisions without academic implications, and there are considerable possibilities of clashes, such as have happened in some American universities. Senate is well represented on the Council, and Council members are, in view of their eminence and other commitments, surprisingly closely in touch with general thinking in the University, and the dyarchy has so far worked well.

The Senate however creates problems in other ways. For the staff it is the place where decisions are made, and in a period when many are concerned with direct democracy, everyone wants to be on it. Senate is thus a body of 400 or so. In general not more than about a quarter attend, and since the expansion of regional staff, the attendance of central academics (who can touch decisions at an earlier stage) has fallen off somewhat. However, a highly controversial agenda late in 1973 brought out nearly 300 people. The trouble with such a large body is not that it cannot take responsible decisions on major issues, but that it cannot within an inevitably limited meeting deal with the routine business, and the nearly routine business (which none the less raises questions in someone's mind), and the not-at-all routine business, which, however well it has been debated elsewhere, is made the subject of debate either by those who have not been involved at an early stage or by those defeated at that stage.

Much depends on the substructure. In early days this was relatively simple. Now it is inordinately complex, and a major review of government structure, which has been dragging on now for many months, does not seem to offer any great simplification. The major problem is a familiar one: larger committees are more representative, smaller committees are more expeditious. None the less, some people have been making some elementary calculations. Members of the academic staff are entitled to two months' vacation and two months' study leave each year. Their working year is thus thirty-five weeks. Assuming an average salary of about £3,500 for an academic, and assuming four full-day Senate meetings in a year, these cost £80 for each to attend, apart altogether from the travel costs and travel time of the regional staff. If all 400 attended, this would come to £32,000 exclusive of travel, mailings of documents and time spent reading those documents. This is the sort of sum whose allocation can cause serious clashes at Planning Board. When you add up all the other boards and committees, you begin to ask, is it worth it? When Planning Board spends an hour debating the allocation of some quite small sum it may well have cost some hundreds of pounds in salaries to debate the matter. I think it essential that everyone has a real say at the grassroots; I think that there are some major policy issues which must be the subject of public debate; but for much else I should be content to leave the decisions to small committees. It was said of one London college that in 1920 it was run by the Principal, Registrar and Head Porter; everyone grumbled, but it was well run. By 1950 it was run by committee upon committee of professors and lecturers; everyone grumbled just as much, and it was no better run. We have not learned that lesson.

Two boards are responsible for most of the internal workings of

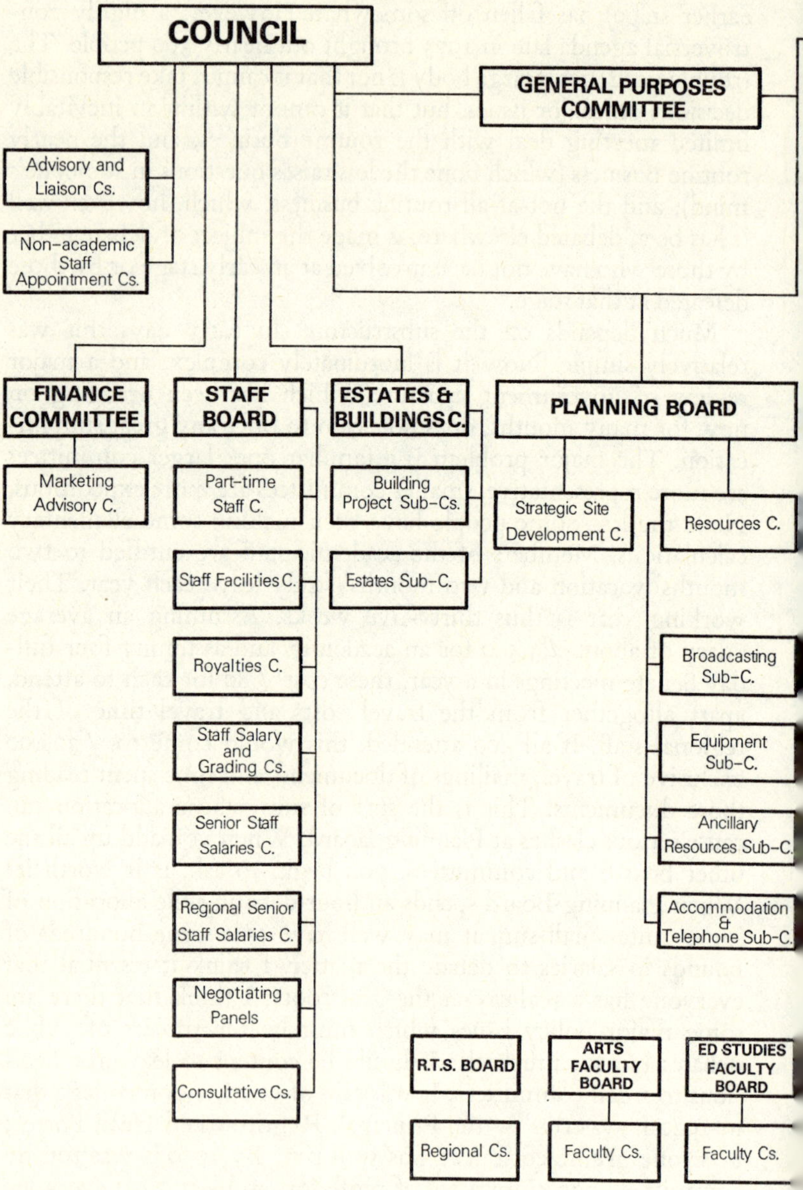

FIG. 5 Proposal from a Study Group for a revised structure for University government, 1973

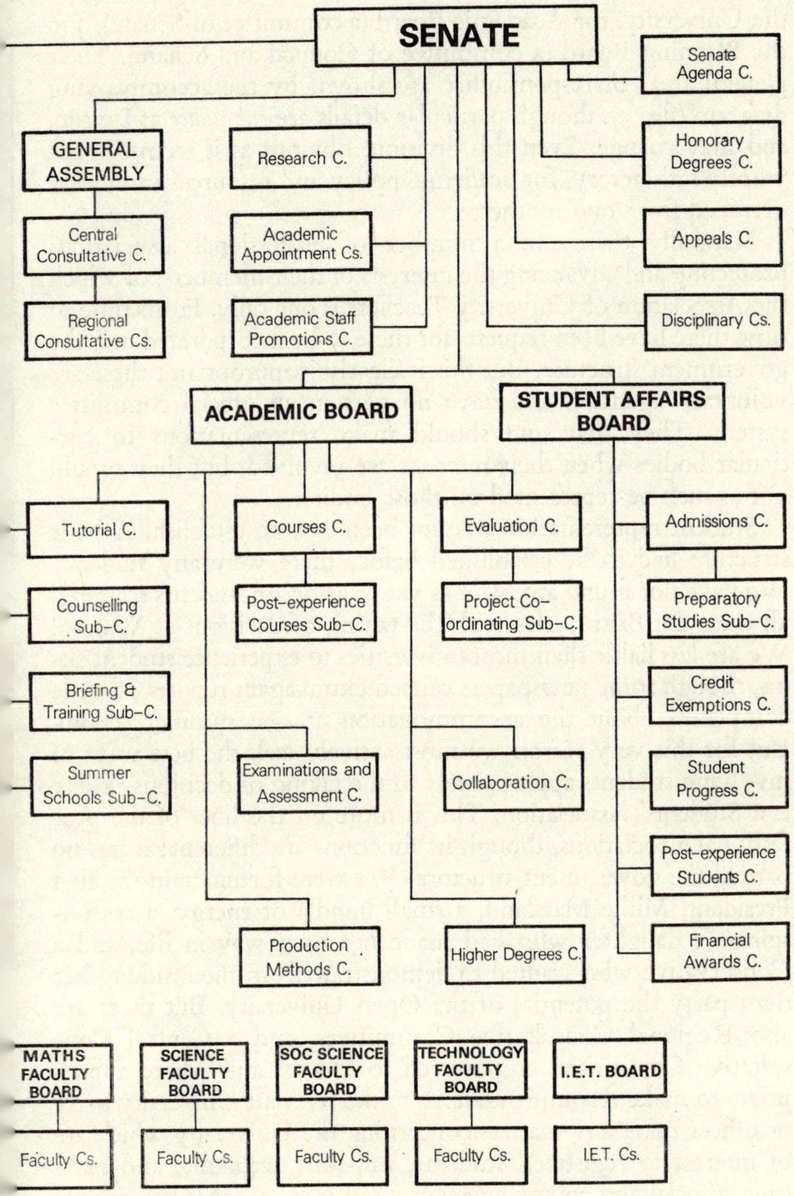
SENATE
Senate Agenda C.
GENERAL ASSEMBLY
Research C.
Honorary Degrees C.
Central Consultative C.
Academic Appointment Cs.
Appeals C.
Regional Consultative Cs.
Academic Staff Promotions C.
Disciplinary Cs.
ACADEMIC BOARD
STUDENT AFFAIRS BOARD
Tutorial C.
Courses C.
Evaluation C.
Admissions C.
Counselling Sub-C.
Post-experience Courses Sub-C.
Project Co-ordinating Sub-C.
Preparatory Studies Sub-C.
Briefing & Training Sub-C.
Credit Exemptions C.
Summer Schools Sub-C.
Examinations and Assessment C.
Collaboration C.
Student Progress C.
Post-experience Students C.
Production Methods C.
Higher Degrees C.
Financial Awards C.
MATHS FACULTY BOARD
SCIENCE FACULTY BOARD
SOC SCIENCE FACULTY BOARD
TECHNOLOGY FACULTY BOARD
I.E.T. BOARD
Faculty Cs.
Faculty Cs.
Faculty Cs.
Faculty Cs.
I.E.T. Cs.

the University, the Academic Board (a committee of Senate), and the Planning Board (a committee of Council and Senate). Their general areas of responsibility are shown by the accompanying diagram (fig. 5), though particular details are *sub judice* as I write, and may change. Even this division, obvious as it seems, is not wholly satisfactory, for academic policy and resources cannot be divorced from one another.

Naturally there are a number of professional associations protecting and advancing the interests of their members, of which the Association of University Teachers is one only. From time to time there have been requests for these to be incorporated into the government structure. But this is clearly inappropriate; these are voluntary agencies, and have no part in an official committee system. They may and should make representations to particular bodies when their interests are involved, but they should not as such be represented on those bodies.

Student representation has not been easy to establish. A basic structure had to be established before there were any students. We have not found any way as yet to associate students scattered all over the British Isles with the taking of decisions at Walton. We are less liable than most universities to experience student sit-ins, though some newspapers carried extravagant reports of some complaints about the accommodation at one summer school. But for this very reason we must actively seek the best ways of involving students appropriately in the taking of decisions. There is a Students' Association. This is more on the lines of the professional associations, though its functions are different; it has no part in the government structure. We were fortunate in the first President, Millie Marsland, a small bundle of energy, a cotton-spinner's daughter who had made her own way in life, and a Conservative who wanted to demonstrate from the inside to her own party the potential of the Open University. But there are also Regional Consultative Committees, and a Central Consultative Committee, empowered to 'discuss and where appropriate to make recommendations to the relevant University body or officer upon any matters concerning the University which are of interest to registered students, full-time academic, and part-time tutorial and counselling staff', and it is here that the student voice can best be heard. There is also the General Assembly, an important forum of opinion, which meets annually, where full-time staff, part-time staff and students are likewise all represented.

Two students serve on the Council, and students also act on disciplinary committees, when these are needed. We are not yet using students as effectively as we should; I have a feeling that there is a particular place for the student who has graduated and is experienced in the system, and who is proceeding to an honours degree.

CHAPTER EIGHT

The Delights and Duties of a Dean

This book began with a statement of a personal approach to the Open University, and it seems sensible that a study of *The Open University from Within* should contain a sketch of the life and work of one dean. For one of the questions I am most frequently asked is 'How do you spend your time?'! 'Are you confined to an office?' and 'Is it all paper-work?' are variants on the same question. The approach must be personal, for the several deans operate in markedly different patterns.

When I was appointed it was clear that to produce anything like an integrated course we would have to work more closely with one another than was normal in other universities. We therefore from an early stage in the history of the University scheduled a weekly faculty board, and my primary function has been to chair this. Members of the faculty have occasionally murmured about the weekly meeting, which no other faculty has, but it is there for two very important reasons. First, if it were not for this weekly meeting we would very easily drift away from one another, particularly when the emphasis is on specialist courses and it would be tempting to mingle merely with those of your own discipline. It is important for the members of the faculty to be in continuous and active cooperation with one another. Second, a weekly meeting means that I have to take very few decisions without consultation with my colleagues. Some of us have been much exercised about the possibilities of genuine democracy, not as casting a vote once every five years, but as a grassroots involvement in the process of taking decisions. If we can't achieve this in the University, it is hard to see how we shall ever achieve it in industry or in the state. It seems to me that the central academics can most effectively influence decisions through the faculty boards, and that major academic issues should first be debated there, as well as matters of particular concern to the faculty, and those niggling details of week-by-week operation which have to be decided somewhere. I unashamedly bring too much to the faculty board rather than too little: for example, matters which might seem the proper concern of a course-team usefully come to faculty board if this prevents the same discussion taking place several times over, or one course-team preempting a discussion which should be wider.

Chairing faculty board is a fascinating and delicate matter. In a community as close-knit as ours, votes are seldom useful. If a motion is carried by 14 votes to 12 it is of little help to anyone. A slightly different board may be divided 12–14 next week. But in any event we cannot go forward if we are as divided as that. My job is therefore to be a Quakerly chairman and seek the sense of the meeting, and, if we are divided, to propose an action on which we can agree. Some people think the dean ought to give a clear lead to faculty board. There are a number of reasons against this. It is undemocratic. It is psychologically wrong: I have sometimes said that the dean's function is to feed in proposals for the faculty to reject so that in finding what they don't want to do they can begin to discover what they do want to do. Of course the dean may have his views as any other member of the board, but he must distinguish these quite clearly from his search, as chairman, for agreement. He has the duty to advise the faculty of the University's determined policies, which must be operated until they are changed. He should have in mind the faculty's earlier decisions, so that there is not constant chopping and changing. He ought to be aware of the views of Council (it was surely a mistake that deans are not on Council), of the problems and opportunities in the operations area, of the implications of views expressed for other faculties. In other words the dean should have a place, and see himself as having a place, in a university structure which operates from the bottom upwards, not from the top downwards. His function is to elicit and coordinate the views of the faculty in such a way that they make sense in the context of the whole university. He is not the man who knows all the answers; it is his job to know as many of the questions as possible. Authoritarian judgement is out. Slickness of operation is less important than openness to other people. Having a firm view of his own is not unimportant, but it is less important than having a clear grasp of what others are saying.

Second in importance to faculty board, and far more time-consuming, is membership of course-teams. When the University started, the faculty board and the foundation course team were identical, and in every faculty the dean was course-team chairman. At the very outset this involved almost daily meetings. Later meetings of the full course-team could be spaced weekly, then fortnightly, then, as the course was completed, monthly, and eventually for 'caretaker purposes' quarterly. To be chairman of a course-team involves eliciting and formulating agreement on the syllabus and its details, the division into blocks of work and working-groups to handle them, the use of outside consultants and contributors, the plans of the working-groups, and the final drafts of written materials, and of broadcast tapes, the spacing and nature of the assignments, and the assignments themselves and tutor-notes to go with them, supplementary materials, and publicity and information about the course, summer-school organization, and the pattern of study-centre tuition (or in later courses day-schools), decisions about 'remakes' of unsatisfactory parts of the course; it involves acting as chairman of the examining board; it involves overall responsibility for the scheduling and the budget; it involves correspondence with tutors and students; close liaison with the operations area; checking all drafts and all proofs; and of course coping with the unpredictable predictable crises. One thing I should say, I am not interested in the minutiae of administration. Scheduling and budgeting control have therefore been exercised in the broadest and simplest, and in my view, the most efficient terms. Budget-control was exercised by limiting every operation to something between a half and three-quarters of the permitted level. In this way one could ignore marginal over-spending, jump on what were obviously excessively long or excessively elaborate units, and yet have a margin for justifiable extras. (BBC expenditure is controlled by the Senior Producers, who seem to me to be using a similar approach.) So with scheduling. Our date for final approval was at least a month ahead of the University's date for handover. Each operation was calculated back from there, and twice as long allowed as was in fact necessary: these would include (working backwards) time for the course-team to read the material; time for the final draft to be typed; time for the author to incorporate criticisms from the working-group; time for those criticisms to reach him; time for the typing of the second draft; time for the writing of the second draft; time for comment on the first draft (which might be very embryonic); time for typing the first draft; time for writing the first draft. In early days we had to allow longer, and material tried out on prospective students had to have an additional eight weeks built into the schedule. Nowadays we find that two drafts are normally enough. Schedules were checked at every course-team meeting and we generally found that that was enough pressure on the laggards. The margins allowed were sufficient to cover minor illness and similar mishaps. One of my rare moments of rebellion was when the Vice-Chancellor's office suddenly required us to fill in a long and complex progress report on every unit at regular intervals. My own system was far simpler, and I had no intention of spending literally hours on an additional and, as far as we were concerned, unnecessary chore. It was a matter of some pride with us that the Arts Faculty did, with a very small number of marginal exceptions, and with a minimum of complex organization or use of the rawhide whip, keep our schedules.

The Arts Faculty operated differently from other faculties in a number of ways. We put more on the working-group and less on the course-team than some faculties. Some faculties have a skeleton course-team for 'maintenance' once a course is complete; we keep the whole course-team in being, with infrequent meetings; we find that all members of the original course-team have to prepare fresh assignments, answer queries, and so on. We had from an early stage considerable overlap of course-teams. Some faculties do not permit any of their members to be on more than one course-team. We took the opposite view. Sensible planning seemed to us to mean entering on the initial discussions and indeed the writing and preparation of second-level courses long before the foundation course was complete, and of third-level courses long before the second-level courses were complete. It took us some time to persuade the University that it was reasonable to be planning courses three years ahead; this is now insisted on for all faculties, and we have the problem of persuading the University that with the amount of time which people must spend on maintenance of existing courses their output of fresh work is reduced to the point where a four-year or even five-year run-in is essential. This means that virtually everyone is on three course-teams, and very likely on more, and is almost certain to be involved in one course which is already completed, another which is in the making, and a third which is in the planning.

A further difference concerned the dean directly. The original Planning Committee picture was of integrated courses up to second-level and specialized courses thereafter. We followed this pattern. This meant that I as dean chaired both the initial second-level course-teams, on *Renaissance and Reformation* and *The Age of Revolutions*. There were a variety of reasons for this. The senior members of the faculty were all beginning to plan their specialist courses; each of them would be chairman of one of the third-level course-teams. To ask any two of them to take over the second-level courses was to introduce an indiscreet note of distinction; it might lead to the slanting of the course in the direction of, or even away from, the chairman's own discipline; and we did not want them to be distracted from their third-level courses by the second level, or *vice versa*. My own specialism of classics was not one of the 'disciplines' in the faculty, but I had some knowledge of literature, history, philosophy and art history from my classical training, and of music, religion and the history of science *per accidens*, as it were. It seemed most sensible that I should chair both these course-teams, although, lacking specialist knowledge in the periods, I was less involved in the writing and, particularly, the broadcasts. This had the added advantage that the work of the two teams was coordinated, and indeed we were able to have a joint examining board to ensure parity of standards. Another advantage lay in the fact that the agreed methods of working in the foundation course, which seemed painless and efficient, were extended for a further year; we hoped that the good points in them might become habitual, while the third-level course-teams might introduce improvements of their own.

I have been a member of all course-teams within the faculty, though I have asked to be excused from attendance at course-team meetings. What I do is to read all course-team material, at least at final draft, and often earlier, and offer comments. Sometimes they are editorial comments, corrections of mis-typings (not very common, for our secretaries are good) and the like, for we wish our material to cause as few problems as possible to the operations area. Sometimes they are the comments of a prospective non-specialist student: perhaps technical terms are being taken for granted, or titles given in French or German, or perhaps the style is polysyllabic or the point unclear. Sometimes they are a faculty comment, a suggestion for a cross-reference to some other point of the faculty's offerings. Just occasionally, to my great satisfaction, I have enough miscellaneous knowledge to correct a fact, suggest an enrichment, propose a visual illustration, question a judgement. This offering of comment from a concerned layman has seemed to us an important aspect of course-preparation.

We expect the dean to play his part in the preparation and presentation of courses with other members of the faculty. I have always, whether as professor or dean, tried to do as much teaching as my colleagues, partly because I enjoy teaching and think it important, partly out of a sense of equity and the realization that we will all pull together better if we really are working as a team and sharing the work. In the Arts Faculty we decided on the principle 'No less—and no more'. In Social Science the dean acted as continuity man for foundation-course television programmes, introducing each and linking it with the course as a whole. There are obvious advantages in this, but in Arts we decided that the dean should be involved in the introductory programme, but otherwise should play the same role as any other member of the team. Similarly over summer school. In Science the dean began at least by paying a brief visit to every summer school. In this way he encountered all the students, and had a first-hand grasp of what was going on. The Arts Faculty decided that the dean should do exactly the same as any other member, one or two weeks as course director or tutor, as he preferred, and as fitted in with the faculty plans. I have in fact worked in a different summer school each year. But by doing the full week I have encountered fewer students but come to know them better.

One other small but not unimportant matter has been the entertainment of colleagues at home. Here my wife has played the leading part; fortunately the years in Nigeria had accustomed her to large parties. In early days it was possible to entertain the whole faculty at once, including our colleagues from the BBC. The faculty has now burst those bounds, but we generally hold two or three buffet-suppers a year so that we all meet in turn from time to time in relaxed informality. Two aspects of these parties have been of some significance. We have always asked wives (or husbands); it seems important to us that work in the University should produce a community in which families feel themselves a part. And all those connected with the faculty, secretaries for example, and editors, and those in media with special responsibility for the work of the faculty, and our admirable reprographer, have shared in these informal occasions as they share in the work of the faculty. Other colleagues have taken similar initiatives, and the result—very important in the early stages—has been a sense of the faculty not as an accidental operation but as a community. In addition to these larger gatherings we naturally from time to time have smaller gatherings also, in which we can get to know one or two couples or individuals better.

Faculty administration has not been particularly onerous because of the excellence of my colleagues. The dean's secretary was conceived as a personal secretary, but from the accidents of personality and history developed early into a faculty administrative secretary. It is a post of considerable responsibility, and is in my view undervalued and underpaid. All faculties were fortunate in the incumbents. There was a curious confusion about administrative support for faculties. We originally interviewed candidates to advise faculties on the visual presentation of material, and appointed a young science teacher, who showed a clear imaginative grasp of the problems and opportunities, to do this for Science. The candidate appointed for Arts was not available for some months. The original concept faded, and the young science-teacher found herself with administrative responsibility, first for two faculties, and then for Arts. These anomalies have since been smoothed out, and there is now the official post of administrative assistant, who is charged with the preparation and execution of faculty business, the production of agenda, preparatory papers, minutes and follow-up papers for the faculty board for instance, as well as the coordination and supervision of the work of the course-assistants. Some deans may like to exercise close control here. I myself do not. I prefer to appoint the right person and leave them to do their own job in their own way.

Equally important was the contribution in early days made by Brian Stone. Stone came to us from Brighton College of Education, a specialist in drama and mediaeval poetry, and a man of strong personality matched with a deep grace of courtesy. It was clear from the first interview that although he loved literature he loved students yet more, and had given much thought to teaching and communication, and was looking forward to pioneering in new methods. He volunteered from the first to take responsibility for the whole area of tuition and counselling, and, not least, the development of summer schools, and did a magnificent job in guiding the work there. All the recommendations of Stone and his committee were of course submitted to faculty board; but, this apart, I did not have to worry my head about this area at all. All the faculties have had their Brian Stones, academics with a primary concern for teaching who have been willing to give time and energy to developing this part of the system. When Brian Stone asked to take study leave, it became clear that the work which he was doing was both indispensable and extremely heavy; no other member of faculty was willing to undertake it. There was therefore need for a new appointment, and we applied for a Sub-Dean. The University committees concerned had still not grasped the nature of the Open University, and the need for people who with high academic qualifications would make their primary professional expertise an area like this. An additional lectureship was authorized, on the understanding that the post of Sub-Dean might rotate in the faculty with an election every three years. We made it equally clear that the successful candidate would be re-elected every three years, and although he would be an academic who would have an academic contribution to make, we were appointing a Sub-Dean, not an additional lecturer, and he would be under no illusions as to the post he was accepting. It was not a satisfactory compromise, and the need for the 'semi-professional' Sub-Dean has come to be widely accepted. We were very fortunate in securing the services of Patrick Berthoud, who had for a time been acting head of the department of English in the University College of Rhodesia, and editor of a fairly radical Catholic journal in that country. He was first-class intellectually, and had worked for a while in the Rhodesian treasury and was an excellent administrator, while at the same time endowed with a firm and eirenic personality—the ideal man for the job.

One administrative chore I kept in my own hands. This was the scheduling of faculty meetings. There were a variety of reasons for this. One was that I rather enjoy this sort of jigsaw puzzle, carry it lightly and do it quickly; it might have been a major operation for anyone else. A second was that it enabled me to weigh and balance conflicting claims within the faculty; everyone, for example, wants meetings when staff tutors are around for their monthly conference, but everyone can't have them. A third was that it enabled me to coordinate the timetable with my own rather complex schedule of University committees. A fourth was that I could guide the faculty by common consent into certain ways of working. The basic principles are fairly simple. It is foolish to require of people a journey into Walton Hall for a single short meeting; it is better to have intensive days with several meetings and as little time wasted as possible. A number of University boards and committees meet on Tuesday or Thursday. The gap of a day gives the secretaries some respite. So meetings of faculty board, sub-committees, course-teams and working groups take place intensively on Tuesdays and Thursdays, with additional meetings once a month on Wednesdays when staff tutors are about. Most members of the faculty will be in every Thursday, and frequently on Tuesdays, but unless they are on other University bodies they are not normally required to be in on other days. Some, of course, do work in their own rooms; others prefer to work at home or in research libraries. It is of vital importance that there is plenty of time for this last; the University library, excellently as it is developing, cannot yet hope to meet all the needs.

Another task, mentioned earlier, is interviews. I have been on, and in fact chaired, every interviewing board (except one while I was away) for posts in the faculty, for posts of every kind except secretarial: academics are kept off these last, perhaps in fear that they might value vital statistics above professional skills. I do not think that other deans have given such priority, but I have been much concerned that we should have in the faculty people of the highest intellectual and professional calibre, and that at the same time we should work together as a faculty. There is of course no attempt to impose a view; the judgement of specialists is always respected, and the dean would not make an appointment by a casting vote but would seek a consensus. The process of selection by interview fascinates me. I don't trust it, and set much store by the evidence of a first-class mind (for administrative as well as academic posts), by experience and voluntary engagement (not least in adult education), and by testimonials from trustworthy sources. But an interview can tell you something. I regard my function as being to set the candidates at ease by exploring some point of personal contact if one is readily available, or by setting them talking on some topic which absorbs them. Otherwise I observe, but am not afraid to put in a challenging question to test response; we don't want yes-men. We set some store on whether candidates have taken the trouble to find out anything about the Open University, or whether this is 'just another job'; equally we discount the well-meaning do-gooder who lacks mental incisiveness. I suppose that with central academic appointments, staff tutors, research assistants, course assistants, and one or two others, despite a very low turnover, we have interviewed for seventy or eighty posts, which is quite time-consuming in the lump. There have not been many disastrously bad appointments, perhaps three in all, and in general we have found the way of easing the square peg out of the round hole, though not always, I fear, in helping to find a square hole.

Another time-consuming but worthwhile occupation is answering students' letters. All deans have this, and it is very important that students shall realize that the University is not a vast impersonal sausage-machine but that we are personally concerned about them. For this reason, even if the letter is an improper attempt to short-circuit the regular University procedures, or if it contains a legitimate query more easily answered by one of my colleagues, I invariably acknowledge it personally to the student concerned and not in a standard time-saving form. The only occasions when I take this sort of short cut is when something has gone wrong with the system, as it is bound to do from time to time, however careful we are. Our students see us not merely as the University of the Second Chance but as the University of the Last Chance, and are liable to agonize over errors of this kind. I sometimes think that they are not very flattering to us, and don't imagine we can have any common sense. When the computer-marked assignment went wrong and everyone received an R (a bad fail grade), we had literally hundreds of letters from the patiently puzzled to (in one case) the anonymously obscene. Here of course our main response was through public announcements. But I answered all the letters, except the anonymous one (which I couldn't), though I had in self-defence to draft one or two standard replies; they were all individually signed. Pleasanter to receive are the letters of personal appreciation and enthusiasm, often after summer school, or at the end of a course. I have one in front of me now, delightfully subscribed 'a happy student', followed by the name. Equally acceptable are the thoughtfully and constructively critical comments we receive in letters. Sometimes there are good reasons for the things they criticize, and it is interesting and important to explain these; sometimes there are substantial and helpful suggestions which we discuss in the course-team or the faculty. Some of the letters are full and fascinating. I have recently had some correspondence with a 73-year-old lady, deaf but indomitable, who described herself as 'a fan of Professor Kettle's' and who was described by the *Daily Mirror* as having 'the fighting spirit of a battleship'. In one letter she gave some account of herself and her various activities, her enjoyment of summer school and her appreciation of all that is done to help deaf students, and said that she had been invited to take part in the David Frost television show, and that she would certainly use the chance to draw attention to the OU. This was followed by another letter in which she recounted her experiences, with 'the fighting spirit of a battleship'. She felt she had been exploited and patronized, and had told David Frost what she thought of him—unfortunately not over the air!

It is important for the dean to meet students where possible. This means travel, but Walton Hall is conveniently situated for this: Oxford, Cambridge, London and Birmingham are not much more than an hour away, Norwich, Leeds and Manchester are not much more than two. Opportunities are varied. Sometimes the dean is invited to a study centre to discuss a particular course, or the work of the faculty; sometimes a study centre has developed a life of its own, as at Aylesbury, and the dean is asked to lecture on an academic topic unconnected with the OU; twice, at Southampton and Edinburgh, I have been asked to preach at an Open University service. Sometimes the encounter is fortuitous, as with the woman who flopped down in the seat opposite me when I was checking some exam papers on a train and said 'Have you got mine there?', or with the policeman at London Airport who stared at me and suddenly said: 'Saw you on telly this morning!'

Another interesting responsibility is welcoming visitors to Walton Hall. The University is attracting visitors of distinction from all over the world, Ministers of Education, Senior Broadcasting officials, Presidents of Universities, academics of all kinds. Some of these want to visit the individual faculties. Then each faculty has its own visitors. It is an important exercise in public relations that the dean or one of his senior colleagues is present for these. Sometimes there are press interviews. In all it is important that the approach of each faculty is fairly represented and clearly understood. Sometimes the invitation is to speak to outside bodies,

Rotary Clubs, educational conferences at home and overseas, the Harrogate Festival, other universities, and the like: this again involves travel.

Deans are naturally involved in University committees. In early days they formed the nucleus of an informal committee, advisory to the Vice-Chancellor, called the Vice-Chancellor's Committee. This offered an informal and lively opportunity for weekly discussion of progress. It was challenged by those who feared a hidden power-structure, enlarged by democratic election, transformed to a General Purposes Committee, and reduced again by the removal of the deans. The result of the absence of the deans from the Council and their elimination from GPC has been to make them more and more inclined to take a faculty view and virtually to prevent them from taking a University view, since they do not know what is going on. For a long period they did not even meet except on boards overweighted with business, but John Sparkes, as Pro-Vice-Chancellor, did an important service by inaugurating occasional meetings of an informal deans' committee. They are of course on Senate, with 400 others, and, as the government structure has developed, on Academic Board and on Planning Board. These boards are lengthy and laborious. I have fortunately acquired some facility for doing two things at once. I have not acquired William Temple's capacity for writing books while chairing meetings, but I can usually read proofs, check course-units, or cope with some of the extraordinary amount of bumff which circulates internally in the University while listening to the routine business of a board or committee.

For this too should not be forgotten as part of the duties of a dean. He must receive each week many hundreds of sheets of paper—in some weeks it must be well into four figures—of reports of boards and committees, statistical surveys, official and unofficial University publications at various stages of draft, press-cuttings, news of activity in the regions, current awareness sheets of recent books; this on top of all that is generated from within the faculty, and all that comes from outside in the way of book catalogues, information from other universities and the like. Even if it is not all read as carefully as it should be, it all has to be sifted.

One thing I have not done, and my fellow-deans have never been more than marginally involved in, and that is canvassing for our own viewpoint or the views of our faculty. It is not that such canvassing is necessarily wrong—and there have been some traumatic confrontations where it has been very important to see that there is an active concern and a clear understanding. It is partly that we are too busy anyway, partly that deans, while morally and constitutionally bound to represent the best interests of their own faculty, ought also to take a larger, 'University' view, partly that those who bear particular responsibility for the structure and procedures of the University should trust that structure and those procedures and not work outside them.

Apart from the boards on which the dean sits *qua* dean, each of us is likely to be playing some role or roles in the life of the University. I was elected Deputy Chairman of Senate. This in itself is not particularly onerous, since all it involves is chairing Senate should the Vice-Chancellor be away. But it carried with it the Deputy-Chairmanship of the Vice-Chancellor's Committee, and later membership of the General Purposes Committee, and participation by rotation with the three Pro-Vice-Chancellors in the Deputy-Chairmanship there. This, apart from adding to the number of meetings, meant that when the Vice-Chancellor was ill for some months I was representing him in these two capacities, without, however, being Deputy Vice-Chancellor. This was a delicate tightrope to walk! During this period I had to represent Senate to Council. But I had never been to Council, and had no idea of its workings. This was unsatisfactory, and I have since been told that I can attend Council *if I like*. I do, but this is not satisfactory either, and it should be both the right and duty of any future Deputy Chairman of Senate to attend Council.

Another area with which I have been involved has been publishing. I was foolish enough to say that the University should have a policy over its relations with the book-trade, and was promptly and inevitably made chairman of the committee to discover what the policy should be, and subsequently chairman of the committee to administer that policy, and of the Advisory Committee on Publishing (by dint of being half Welsh I'm also on the Advisory Committee for Wales). (Advisory committees are an important public relations exercise; the Advisory Committee on Publishing brings together representatives of the Publishers Association, the Booksellers Association, the Library Association, the Society of Authors and other similar bodies.) I have already written of our opportunities in this area. It has been fascinating to help form them. In the early days I seemed to be being lunched by every publisher in London—it was very bad for the figure!—who was anxious to explore work with the Open University. When taking hard decisions subsequently I sometimes felt like the voter in the bad old days: 'I've eaten their food, I've drunk their beer, I've ridden in their coaches, and I've voted agin' 'em.' It would be hard to overpraise the cooperation and helpfulness of the book-trade, and one of my gladder moments was to meet the representative of the Booksellers Association at the first graduation ceremony, and see the proprietary pride he was taking in the occasion. Across the next few years we expect to see considerable developments from the Open University Press, without losing the healthy relation we have built up with other publishers.

There have been other *ad hoc* calls. One I remember without pleasure was an appeal committee to hear the case of a part-time counsellor who had been relieved of his office on the grounds of dereliction of duty. It was not expected to last long, but the counsellor concerned was a member of the legal profession who seemed to have decided to use this as an opportunity for putting in some professional practice. His case was unimpressive, but he certainly spun it out.

The University is naturally asked from time to time to provide a representative to serve on some other body, and deans have been asked to help with this. I have served on the Governing Board of Milton Keynes College of Education. Unfortunately their meetings almost always coincide with either Senate or Council, so I have not been much help at governors' meetings. But we have fostered an experimental scheme of collaboration between the University and the College: the College provides the University with a study centre, which I have visited, we try to attend and support public occasions there, and I have been privileged to run a madrigal group there, so getting personal contact with students and staff. The Principal sometimes discusses College business with me, and I have also personal contact with a number of his colleagues. This sort of liaison strikes me as of great importance for the University itself, apart from any contribution which we can make to other educational institutions.

One other responsibility remains of a different kind. We are naturally primarily concerned with the building up of the Open University and its teaching system. But all academics have a responsibility within their own subject. I have tried to ensure that I from time to time can develop my own research and writing, and welcome the opportunity, for example, to speak to the annual meeting of the Classical Association, to deliver the Kinchin-Smith Memorial Lecture, to address the Vergilian Society, to speak to a sixth-form classics conference at Ealing. In addition to this specific academic responsibility, there is a wider responsibility in citizenship. How and where this is exercised is a matter for the individual. The Dean of Education, for example, is a member of the General Synod of the Church of England; one of the mathematicians is a leading member of the British Humanist Association; others of my colleagues are engaged in local government or national politics. I regard my chairmanship of the British Council of Churches Education Department, my sharing in the editorial responsibility for *Reconciliation Quarterly*, my acting as a rapporteur for a churches' commission on Nonviolent Action, my chairmanship of the meetings which led to the formation of a Religious Education Council, my membership of the national executive of UNA, as a natural outcome of my position as a senior academic, as a compliment to the Open University, and as among other things a piece of public relations for the Open University. Plainly, the exacting nature of the Open University limits the amount of public service which it is possible to give. But it would be a sorry day if it were not possible to give any at all.

There has not in all this been much time for holidays. It's not that any one of us has been indispensable, but that the pile-up of work on one's return undoes the good that the break has brought. Better, until this changes, to take the opportunity of passing recreation while keeping the work in hand. A week-end away walking in the Welsh mountains, the occasional game of cricket for the MCC, a couple of days at Glyndebourne, an hour after supper listening to a gramophone record, an evening picking up the threads with longstanding friends, visitors from Nigeria or America—all these can work wonders. I have valued greatly my madrigal group. We meet on Thursdays at 6.0 p.m. This works well. This is the one day on which I am invariably at the University; I can give my singers a firm commitment. Thursdays can be trying. They can end with a residue of unfinished work, which could, but should not, keep me at Walton to all hours. The madrigal group has meant that I have to be away by about a quarter to six, and that I can forget all the day's trials in the exquisite sensitivity of Dowland and Gibbons, Weelkes and Morley.

Is there a constant pattern? Not really. I'm always in Walton on Thursdays with a full schedule; the first half-hour goes in dictating letters, which otherwise have to be fitted into odd moments. I'm usually in on Tuesdays, unless Council or some other official engagement takes me to London. The number of days spent at Walton varies with University committees, official visitors and the like; it is usually two, three or four, but I try to avoid it becoming five, or no real work would ever be done. I hereby pay the warmest possible tribute to those secretaries who have coped with varied and complex dictation at irregular times, carried out against the clock, in addition to their remarkable achievements in palaeography in deciphering and transcribing articles and course-units and books and memoranda of all sorts. There are few weeks when I do not go to London at least one day. This may be for an official University body, or for the making of a radio or television programme (which may of course involve more than one appearance), or to represent the University in some capacity, or in connection with some form of public activity, or simply to consult a library. I invariably use trains except for cross-country journeys (the libraries in Cambridge and Oxford are far more accessible by car). These visits to London, together with the longer journeys, give the possibility of reading. With them I just about keep abreast of periodicals and of my colleagues' course-units. I had thought that I was doing little reading outside these. But when I added up the books I was reading on train journeys, in libraries, in baths, while listening to records, in bed, and at other fleeting moments, I found that in the fourteen months from October 1972 to November 1973 I had read rather more than 300 books, varying in length from *Anna Karenina* to an extended pamphlet. I wouldn't promise to answer an examination on them all!

There are two important aspects of the work, which prevent it from becoming intolerably burdensome. One is that it is so varied; a change is as good as a rest, and I can work a sixteen-hour day provided I get eight hours' sleep and there's plenty of variety in the work. The other is that it is in quite a large measure personal; it consists of communication with a widely differing range of people. This is important. I have resisted putting letters on tape, because the personal contact is vital for me, and perhaps for the secretaries as well. Two minutes with the sub-dean will achieve more than many memos, and leave me, and perhaps him, refreshed instead of jaded. There remains too little time for some of the things we would wish to do. We do not spend enough time in informal conversation with colleagues in other faculties. A few minutes' private talk could clear away a deal of misunderstanding. Late in 1973 the Vice-Chancellor organized a residential 'think-tank' about the present and future of the University. Pro-Vice-Chancellors and deans were all there, and other senior representatives of the University to the number of thirty. Two things impressed me particularly. One was the remarkable measure of basic agreement. The other was the value of the informal meal-time conversations in helping us to understand one another. All in all it has been a tremendously exciting experience to share in. *Haec olim meminisse iuvabit*, and to say of them *quorum pars minima fui.*

CHAPTER NINE

Retrospect and Prospect

That the Open University has come to stay seems beyond doubt. That it has had a success, not merely far beyond that expected by its severest critics, but far beyond that dreamed by its most hopeful advocates seems also true. That it has not always lived up to its pretensions is sure. There *is* dull teaching, there *are* shoddy television programmes, the vaunted integration is sometimes no more than papering over the cracks, there has been quarrelsomeness as well as cooperation. The achievements remain. Above all, the University is now accepted.

The University in the end will be judged by its graduates; one of the early anxieties of students was whether their degree would be recognized as a 'proper' degree. Obviously this will vary from one employer to another. At least in the teaching profession and the civil service we know that it is recognized as a proper degree. No one would pretend that an OU graduate will acquire the same sort of specialist expertise which a graduate acquires in a traditional Oxbridge special honours school. He will have other qualities, not less important. Some of them are intellectual, an ability to master a broad range of material, a capacity for seeing a subject in its context, for making comparative judgements, for taking a synoptic view. Others are moral and personal; anyone who completes an OU degree has enormous powers of application, determination, persistence and resilience. There are signs that employers are honouring these qualities; one of my acquaintances among the first graduates was immediately appointed to a post of special responsibility.

One further factor must be remembered. The OU is not adding to the number of graduates unemployed in the obvious sense. Our students fall into five categories. Some will remain within their present posts and be more effective within them for their study. Some will remain within their present career-structure, and will hope for, and be better qualified to receive, promotion within that career-structure. Some will be hoping to change their job altogether; they are already in one job, and they do not need to leave that until they are appointed to the other. Some, retired people for example, and others for whom the courses are primarily a constructive leisure activity, are not seeking employment through their degree. There remains a fifth group, including housewives, who are certainly hoping for posts they do not now hold; they will be seeking posts anyway; they will be better qualified when they do so. But, for the most part, they won't be swelling the dole queues. And they are a minority among our students.

Are there sufficient students to justify the Open University continuing on its present scale, or larger? I find it impossible to doubt. The careful survey of the Planning Committee indicated a potential field of at least 250,000. If our intake remains at or around 15,000 it will be sixteen years before we have begun to clear away the backlog: and by that time there will be a fresh backlog. The number of applicants rises without difficulty to twice the number we can take; if it lags, extra expenditure on publicity seems to rally it. Furthermore, in the last year or two a high proportion of those qualified for places at universities have not been taking them up. Many of these will almost certainly come to feel the need of a university education and a university qualification. They will then be in full-time employment, and perhaps with families. They have of course the normal qualifications, but if we are really an Open University we do not hold it against an applicant that he is qualified any more than that he is unqualified. Apart from this group there are signs that a number of professions, which have in the past welcomed non-graduates, will become all-graduate in the predictable future, and many in these will wish and indeed be required to have a degree; such are the teaching profession and the civil service if I read the signs rightly.

Can we increase our working-class enrolment? One of our students, married to a stevedore and living in dockland, wrote a very sensible letter to the Students' Association journal *Sesame* about her conversations with friends and neighbours. Many had never heard of the Open University, but once they knew about it thought it a good idea—for other people. There seemed little incentive to move in that direction. The costs involved were no deterrent, nor tiredness at the end of the day, nor the pub (which they said was only a substitute for something better to do). This problem of incentive was the major obstacle. But a second was the assumptions of entry-behaviour. For despite all our profession of openness our courses really are from the first geared in to the grammar school student. We assume not merely literacy, but experience in continuous reading and continuous writing, not merely numeracy, but a considerable amount of sophisticated numeracy. They looked at course-material, and thought they would spend all their time looking up words in dictionaries. A100 they described as 'strictly for the birds'—meaning eccentrics, hippies, students and beatniks. Yet many of these men and women are great characters and philosophers in their way.

All this points to a number of questions. Should we offer, or encourage others to offer, preparatory courses? Can we do this without either disappointing those who take them successfully or offending against the principle of open admission? Can we do it in the period between registration and the start of courses? Should we lower the assumed entry-behaviour at foundation level? Can we do this without lowering the standards of the degree? Are we perhaps, for all our pioneering enterprise, really in the end hidebound by traditional concepts? Does the intellectual quality and development appropriate for a degree really depend on continuity of reading and writing? Would it be possible to present material of university standard in the form of tabloid paragraphs and comic strips, and to accept answers in note-form or perhaps even given orally on tape? Or would this devalue the degree? These and similar questions we must face. Meanwhile there is the problem of publicity among, communication with and motivation of the blue-collar workers.

One interesting experiment has been carried out in San Diego. This is a series of popularly written but serious academic syndicated articles in the press, accompanied by questions to which readers were invited to send in answers. They were promised that these answers would receive proper comment and assessment. As a result, people who had written in out of curiosity found 'I can do this' and became absorbed in what they were doing, and suitable people from among them have been encouraged to study for a degree. We might be able to do something similar.

There are perhaps more fundamental questions still. We have learned from Ivan Illich, and from Paolo Freire (to whom the Open University gave an honorary degree) something of the concept of deschooling. Does this include 'deuniversitizing'? Are we in fact still subserving a familiar social situation? Ought we to be seeking to do something different? Ought we to be starting from the beginning rather than the end, from where people are rather than where we want them to be? Ought we to be examining local needs, grassroots needs, community needs? Might this lead to a very different concept of a university, perhaps not primarily focused on a degree programme, perhaps involving a different sort of degree programme, certainly with a much more diversified and practical range of offerings? For until we find new ways of motivation we shall continue to attract primarily those who have already had some taste of advanced education. Two-thirds of our applicants are qualified. Many have enjoyed some post-secondary education. The calculation has been made that out of every million adults 180,000 have received some post-secondary education, and 820,000 have not. Unless the pattern of our applicants changes we can expect that over a period of twenty years we shall receive 30,000 applications from each million, and 20,000 of them will come from the 180,000 and only 10,000 from the 820,000. Perhaps this is right. Perhaps we should meet the continuing need in the semi-qualified area as our priority. But it leaves one a little uneasy.

What of the tortured question of the admission of the eighteen to twenty-one age-group? I have already touched on this in its historical context. In 1970 it looked as if the pressure on the universities from qualified applicants in this group would be impossible to meet. When the Conservatives came into power they began to ask whether we could help. I remember an informal conversation with William van Straubenzee in which he asked me directly about this. I said that I could see nothing against the admission of eighteen-year-olds in principle, but could wish that the government would let us get off the ground before bringing pressure here—while recognizing that their problem was immediate and could not wait. This apart, we were determined on two things—that admission of eighteen-year-olds should not interfere with our primary function of serving the mature student, and would have to be financed separately, and that if we admitted eighteen-year-olds it could not be on a basis of normal entrance qualification, but would have to be open to all. The government behaved with utter propriety, and no direct pressures were applied, but we were asked what our general contribution would be to higher education in the 1970s and it was clear that the eighteen-year-olds were in ambush round the corner! A complicating factor was that our system was designed for the mature student; it was not at all clear how far it would be valid for the normal undergraduate. So we offered to mount a pilot-scheme in 1974 and 1975, admitting 500 eighteen-year-olds in each of those years, some highly qualified, some marginally qualified, and some unqualified, and test the possibilities. This is being done, but the pressures are in fact off the universities, and, unless there is a startling change, it is unlikely that anything will come of it.

This is not to say that we have no function with the under-21s. One obvious possibility, already mentioned, is that holders of the Dip.H.E., some of whom will be under twenty-one, might leave college and take a job, immediately registering for two further credits with the Open University. Another possibility is that the Open University might cooperate with colleges of education anywhere in the country in offering a degree programme. A pilot experiment is in progress with our neighbours, the Milton Keynes College of Education; the neighbourliness has obvious advantages in the possibilities of immediate consultation, but it also means that the situation is atypical. The University has been exploring the possibilities of a kind of troika. It is impossible for us to validate courses in the colleges, partly because we have not the resources to do so, partly because many courses (e.g. in languages) will be in areas where we have no specialists. So we have been looking at the possibility of degrees in which Open University courses play a part, and the college courses receive validation by the Council for National Academic Awards (CNAA). One problem is that our academic year coincides with the calendar year not the college year, but this is a complicating factor rather than an impossible barrier.

In fact there are many possible patterns of cooperation with existing institutions, and it seems fairly certain that some of these will be developed in the next ten years. The Soviet Union has produced engineering graduates by tuition through radio and correspondence, with a one-year residential period at Moscow or Leningrad at the end of it. But this is not the only mix possible, or necessarily the best. Some university students would benefit by leaving university earlier and completing their degree while doing a practical job; others would be helped by a period of full-time employment, while keeping up their studies, in the middle of their course. The OU could contribute in any of these ways, and different schemes of cooperation might be worked out with different universities and polytechnics. In particular, I suspect that some of the future developments in science at the OU may depend on working with technical colleges and polytechnics which will provide laboratory-based courses. This may exclude our shepherd on the island of Mull, but we shall have at some point to decide whether every course must be accessible to every conceivable student (already prisoners cannot take S100), and whether we are justified in holding back a majority because of the more isolated individuals.

Geoffrey Holister, the first Dean of Technology, was asked by his former colleagues on his appointment why he was putting his whole career in jeopardy by joining the Open University. He replied: 'If we succeed in five years it will be your careers which are at risk.' This was of course intended as a paradox, but a challenging one.

The Open University does in fact interact with other universities and institutions of higher education in a number of ways. First, never in the history of higher education has so much trouble been taken over the quality of teaching. Students in other universities can read our materials, they can watch and listen to our broadcasts, and they are not going to be fobbed off by the shoddy and second-rate which so often passes for university teaching. It is not that we are any better than others; most of us came out of some other university, and have come to realize how inadequate was our former teaching. There we received no training; here we have educational technologists breathing down our necks and asking awkward questions. There we knew we could get away with a certain amount, for our colleagues and seniors did not sit in on our classes; here all our teaching is exposed to every professor in the world. There our teaching was never tested and seldom criticized; here it receives the candid comments of students before it is finalized. There we never seriously discussed our teaching with our colleagues; here all our teaching is thrashed out with our colleagues, though it remains individual and personal. Standards of university teaching are mostly low. I have suffered lecturers inaudible beyond the front row, lecturers who hop birdlike from bough to bough pecking here and there, lecturers who charge through at 100 m.p.h., lecturers of whom I haven't understood a word, lecturers who have copied their notes verbatim from a textbook, lecturers who would never think of raising a question or issuing a challenge. It does none of us harm to look at our aims and objectives, and to evaluate our methods in the light of those. If we can do something to raise the standards of teaching throughout higher education it will be well worthwhile.

Second, it is possible for universities to make direct use of our methods and even our material. In this country we do not often have very large classes but we waste a lot of time in using fairly impersonal methods for teaching relatively small numbers. It is doubtful if a seminar technique has much use for classes numbering over twenty; some would say twelve, or even six. So we lecture, and the number of good lecturers is small, and the number of bad lecturers is large. How much better to use Open University methods and, where apposite, Open University material! I must repeat a point I made in the first chapter. Many critics of the Open University have insisted that personal encounter between teacher and taught is the essence of higher education. Good. It is worth going on to ask how many students ever experience it. Not many general students. Not many honours students in large departments. By the use of Open University methods and materials for some of the teaching, we could free staff for the genuine personal encounters with individuals and small groups which at present are a minor or non-existent part of the week for many.

In this respect I still think that our ultimate impact may be greatest when our experience and methodology is applied in the Third World. There the need is greatest, and its potentiality lies not merely in courses of university quality, but in sixth-form courses, in the concept of an Open School, in adult education which has nothing to do with conventional university studies. For we have three things immediately to offer: our experience in teaching adults, our experience in teaching large numbers of people simultaneously, and far more inexpensively than could be done by other means, and the care we have taken over the structuring of effective teaching. We have been less good in meeting the underprivileged where they are, less good in conceiving functions which do not lie firmly within those of the traditional university. But if the Third World, perhaps with help from UNESCO, can start by bringing together their understanding of need with our understanding of method, they will devise something new, and we shall learn from them.

We need to. The two things which frighten me most about the Open University is that all our revolutionary achievement, which is real and startling, has been carried out within the framework of traditional Western higher education, and that the heterodoxies which we have produced have within three years of operation spawned a tyrannical orthodoxy of their own.

Partly this was inevitable. If we had not been somewhat within the present system, we would never have received the backing to start. And it is our success which has created its own orthodoxy. We cannot at this stage seek radical change; we have barely started on our first journey. It is unlikely that the next ten years will see a very different pattern. Slowly, more courses in the science-based areas will become available. There may be new areas of study, perhaps even new faculties. I should certainly like to see the number of students doubled, and would regard this as a major pressure to bring on those who hold the key to the strong-room. We shall be hampered by the present lack of mobility in university teaching, and by the very loyalty of our staff; if this continues we shall have to organize extended exchanges (one year is not enough) with other universities, so that we can feed new ideas to them, and they to us.

Hopefully, as they say in America, there will be enough of us open to fresh ideas and new thinking. And history often has surprises round the corner. Perhaps some of our own graduates may join the staff, and bring new vision. Who knows?

Meantime the last word can remain with an American visitor. He said: 'I thought I was visiting a country which was still living in the nineteenth century—and I found myself confronted with the university of the twenty-first century.'

Index